THE SHORT LIFE & CURIOUS DEATH OF FREE SPEECH IN AMERICA

ALSO BY ELLIS COSE

Democracy, If We Can Keep It

The End of Anger

Bone to Pick

The Envy of the World

The Best Defense

The Darden Dilemma

Color-Blind

A Man's World

The Rage of a Privileged Class

A Nation of Strangers

The Press

THE SHORT LIFE & CURIOUS DEATH OF FREE SPEECH IN AMERICA

ELLIS COSE

An Imprint of HarperCollinsPublishers

THE SHORT LIFE AND CURIOUS DEATH OF FREE SPEECH IN AMERICA.

For information, address HarperCollins Publishers, 195 Broadway, New York, NY 10007.

HarperCollins books may be purchased for educational, business, or sales promotional use. For information, please email the Special Markets Department at SPsales@harpercollins.com.

FIRST HARPERCOLLINS PAPERBACK EDITION PUBLISHED IN 2021

Designed by SBI Book Arts, LLC

Library of Congress Cataloging-in-Publication Data is available upon request.

ISBN 978-0-06-299972-6

21 22 23 24 25 LSC 10 9 8 7 6 5 4 3 2 1

For Lee and Elisa, and in memory of Nelson

CONTENTS

THE SHORT LIFE & CURIOUS DEATH OF FREE SPEECH IN AMERICA

INTRODUCTION

DEFENDING HATEFUL SPEECH

No one expected their words to be enlightening or their tone harmonious. Hatred rarely comes in such flavors. It spills out as an ugly, incoherent mess infused with the rotten odor of willful ignorance. And so it was with the Nazi wannabes—self-styled white supremacists determined to make their mark on the world, committed to convincing anyone who might listen that their superiority was both evident and inevitable.

The setting was downtown Charlottesville, Virginia, August 2017. Their mission was unity—of like-minded hatemongers. Their leader, Jason Kessler, was a thirty-three-year-old who lived with his parents and had once supported Barack Obama. He had learned that many demographers thought whites would eventually become a minority race in the United States. That news was so unsettling that Kessler remade himself into a white-rights activist: "It's one thing to have immigration, but to the point where they [nonwhites] overwhelm the host population is not right." He styled himself as "a civil and human rights advocate, focused on the Caucasian demographic" in the mode of "Jesus Christ or Mahatma Gandhi." His Unite the Right rally, observed the *Christian Science Monitor*, "was supposed to be the movement's coming out party, an emergence from the shadows of internet chat rooms into the national spotlight."

Kessler was inspired in part by fellow University of Virginia graduate and white supremacist Richard Spencer who, in May 2017, led a band of racists in Charlottesville chanting "Russia is our friend" and "Blood and soil," a Nazi-inspired slogan. Why they were enamored of Russia is anyone's guess; I presume it had something to do with President Trump. The reason for the Nazi chant was evident; they thought it allowed them to channel the spirit of General Robert E. Lee, who had abandoned the US Army in a doomed quest to preserve race-based slavery in the South. Charlottesville's leaders recently had voted to remove Lee's statue from the downtown park that no longer carried his name. Spencer and his crew opposed that effort and everything they thought it implied, including hostility to the legacy of whiteness. "What brings us together is that we are white, we are a people, we will not be replaced," Spencer told the acolytes he had summoned to Charlottesville.

The Loyal White Knights of the Ku Klux Klan were similarly motivated by the perceived threat to American whiteness. Its members—fifty strong—converged on Charlottesville that July to march around and shout "White power" as hundreds of counterprotesters responded with "Racists go home."

How did the mad ravings of a bunch of mentally disturbed, intellectually confused, racially paranoid misfits end up spurring a national debate over the limits of free speech, the meaning of the First Amendment, and the moral obligation of the president of the United States? One reason is that—despite Kessler's efforts to cast himself as the Martin Luther King Jr. of white rights—the rally engendered fears of made-for-TV-scale violence.

As news of the event spread, and some sense of its size became clear, several local businesses announced they would temporarily close out of concern for the safety of their customers and employees. The University of Virginia, located in Charlottesville, asked students to stay away.

Many rally participants showed up armed with rifles and other deadly weapons (thanks to Virginia's open carry laws). Indeed, even before the rally's scheduled noon start time, Kessler's congregation had ignited so much hostility and ugliness that local authorities labeled the gathering an "illegal assembly" and ordered participants to leave.

In the end, the racist, anti-Semitic hate-fest caused three deaths. Two of the dead were state troopers. Berke Bates and H. Jay Cullen, assigned to monitor the gathering from the sky, died when their helicopter crashed. The third victim was Heather Heyer, a thirty-two-year-old paralegal.

James Alex Fields Jr., a twenty-year-old Adolf Hitler fanatic from Ohio, killed Heyer by intentionally plowing his car into a crowd of counterprotesters—injuring some nineteen people in addition to Heyer, who died from "blunt-force injury" to her chest.

Following the tragedy, Donald Trump famously condemned the "hatred, bigotry, and violence on many sides."

His words provoked a controversy that went on for months as Trump proved incapable of criticizing the racist mob without also condemning those who opposed it. Heyer's mother, Susan Bro, was so sickened by the president's words that she refused to take his condolence call. "I'm sorry. After what he said about my child," Bro told CNN, and added, incredulous: "I saw an actual clip of him at a press conference equating the protesters . . . with the KKK and the white supremacists."

James Fields's lawyers sought mitigation by stressing his history of mental illness. A psychologist testified that he had been diagnosed with bipolar disorder at the age of six and later with schizoid personality disorder. His lawyers also delved into his childhood traumas, which included coping with the murder of his grandmother by his grandfather, who had subsequently killed himself. "James's mental illness causes him to lose emotional and behavioral control in stressful situations," said his attorneys, who claimed he had taken himself off his meds when he was eighteen, meaning he was medically untethered when he murdered Heyer. After pleading guilty, Fields received two life sentences—one in state court and the other in federal court.

Even with Fields confined to prison, questions raised by Heyer's murder—and the rally that caused it—reverberated. Trump's troubling insistence on calling bullying bigots "very fine people" was perhaps inevitable given his need to placate a base that contains more than its share of people like David Duke, the former Ku Klux Klan grand wizard who promoted the rally as an effort to "take our country back" and who, after Heyer's murder, thanked Trump via tweet for his "honesty &

courage to tell the truth." Duke also tweeted, "This is why WE LOVE TRUMP and WHY the FAKE NEWS MEDIA HATES TRUMP. He brings to light what the lying, Fake News Media Won't. The truth is the media covers up horrific numbers of racist hate crimes against White people!"

But putting the president and his behavior aside for the moment, what about the free speech community—the civil libertarians who successfully fought in court for Kessler's right to hold his rally in downtown Charlottesville? The city had wanted to move Kessler's parade of bigotry to another park, one farther from the heart of town that officials claimed would be easier to police. But Kessler had said no; and the American Civil Liberties Union, along with a local outfit called the Rutherford Institute, had sued the city on Kessler's behalf.

Following the event, the ACLU was heavily criticized—and also lauded—for standing up for the racist rabble-rousers. Glenn Greenwald, best known for reporting on US surveillance programs brought to light by whistleblower Edward Snowden, forcefully defended the ACLU. Civil liberties advocates, he argued, "defend the rights of those with views we hate in order to strengthen our defense of the rights of those who are most marginalized and vulnerable in society."

Others were not so sure. *The Guardian* newspaper reported on an erosion in "the belief that the KKK and other white supremacist organisations are operating within the bounds of acceptable political discourse—rather than as, say, terrorist organisations—and therefore have a moral right to be heard."

Jessica Clarke, a law professor at Vanderbilt University

Law School, pointed to studies showing that bigots routinely hid behind free speech arguments as a cover for racism. Highly prejudiced people, she noted, "were less likely to voice First Amendment objections when the threatened speech was race-neutral, suggesting their free speech concerns were more about the freedom to express racist prejudice than free speech in general."

Legal scholar Laura Weinrib noted that the ACLU had never blindly supported free speech but had done so in the fight for a better society; and she wondered whether "a dogged commitment to free speech" was still the best strategy for an organization pursuing social justice: "The balances have shifted dramatically since the 1930s. In recent years, nearly half of 1st Amendment victories have gone to corporations and trade groups challenging government regulation. Free speech has served to secure the political influence of wealthy donors. Labor's strength has plummeted, and the Supreme Court is poised to recognize a 1st Amendment right of public sector employees to refuse to contribute to union expenses. Long-settled principles of American democracy are newly vulnerable, and hate has found fertile terrain."

Even Susan Herman, president of the ACLU, questioned whether old assumptions about free speech still applied: "We need to consider whether some of our timeworn maxims—the antidote to bad speech is more speech, the marketplace of ideas will result in the best arguments winning out—still ring true in an era when white supremacists have a friend in the White House."

Leslie Mehta, the young black attorney who was legal director of the ACLU of Virginia when it took the Kessler case, seemed confident, when I interviewed her in the aftermath of Heyer's death, that she had made the right decision. "There were certainly lots of conversations between myself and the executive director. There were a lot of revisions back and forth with briefs and having discussions about potential implications, but nobody has a crystal ball and no one [knew] exactly what [would] ultimately happen. I do think that the First Amendment has to mean something. And at the time, it was my understanding . . . that there was no evidence that there would be violence."

Mehta, a native of Woodland, North Carolina, is intimately familiar with the South and with the United States' legacy of brutal racial oppression. She went to historically black Howard University School of Law because of its reputation for creating lawyers devoted to "social activism and social justice." But she also is adamantly committed to the idea of free speech. "I think one of the reasons why free speech is so important to me is because . . . it exposes what you disagree with. And for me, I think it's important to hear things like our president saying . . . 'Well, there are good people on both sides.'"

Mehta also thought it was important to consult with her mother and her ninety-two-year-old grandmother as she proceeded with the Kessler case. Her grandmother, she confided, "never said that she fully agreed or disagreed [with Mehta taking the case], but she did not think that I was wrong."

As anyone trying to understand the Charlottesville fiasco quickly discovers, the issue of speech—particularly in a society polluted by racism and largely defined by economic inequality—is endlessly complex. So let me begin this journey with a brief exploration of how the US came to embrace such a broad notion of free speech, and let's look at some decisions made in its name.

• • •

We tend to think our current conception of free speech has been around essentially since the beginning of the republic. In truth, our firm and collective embrace of the First Amendment is a relatively recent phenomenon.

The Constitution was drafted at a time when the Founders had rejected foreign tyranny. They were wary of the potential power of a centralized state. So the Bill of Rights was a balancing act, weighing not only the rights of individuals versus government in general but also the rights of states versus the federal government.

Indeed, at the time the Bill of Rights was ratified, the First Amendment did not apply to the states. As legal scholar David Yassky has pointed out, the Constitution's guarantee of free speech was "quite weak—at least to contemporary eyes. A citizen in 1800 had no absolute right to free speech; if the speech-restricting law was a state law, the Constitution was silent."

Eventually that changed, and that had a lot to do with the Civil War, the end of slavery, the Fourteenth Amendment, and assorted court decisions. But even after the Reconstruction era, free speech, as we understand it today, was nothing but an aspiration, which is one reason that southern states could effectively outlaw agitation for abolition.

Free speech is very much an invention of the twentieth century. And that concept of speech is very idealistic, inextricably linked to the notion that in the competition of ideas, good ideas generally crowd out bad.

That argument received its most famous articulation in a 1927 case: *Whitney v. California*. At its center was Charlotte Anita Whitney, a wealthy California blueblood convicted of joining the Communist Party. She argued that her prosecution violated the Constitution. The Supreme Court unanimously disagreed. But even in disagreeing with her position, Louis Brandeis (joined by Oliver Wendell Holmes Jr.) produced a brilliant and eloquent exegesis on the potential of free speech to enact social change:

> Those who won our independence believed that the final end of the State was to make men free to develop their faculties, and that, in its government, the deliberative forces should prevail over the arbitrary. They valued liberty both as an end, and as a means. They believed liberty to be the secret of happiness, and courage to be the secret of liberty. They believed that freedom to think as you will and to speak as you think are means indispensable to the discovery and spread of political truth; that, without free speech and assembly, discussion would be futile; that, with them, discussion affords ordinarily adequate protection against the dissemination of noxious doctrine.

As Brandeis saw it, free speech was virtually a sacred right and an awesomely powerful force that would expose "falsehood and fallacies" and "avert . . . evil by the processes of education." Hence, the remedy to bad speech was "more speech, not enforced silence."

That piece of writing has been deemed one of the most important commentaries ever crafted on the First Amendment. But Brandeis assumed something that has not been borne out by facts, which is that the better argument would generally win. He also assumed that relevant people on all sides of a question were equally capable of being heard and that skeptics were interested in listening.

That fallacy continues to inform the thinking of those who see speech as inherently self-correcting.

Facebook founder and chief executive Mark Zuckerberg waded into the debate after Facebook green-lighted the running of blatantly dishonest ads by political candidates. Zuckerberg's rational was that, in the interest of free speech, he would censor nothing—including obvious lies—that appeared in ads run by politicians.

In a speech in October 2019 at Georgetown University, Zuckerberg explained his reasoning: "Frederick Douglass once called free expression 'the great moral renovator of society.' He said, 'Slavery cannot tolerate free speech.' Civil rights leaders argued time and again that their protests were protected free expression, and one noted: 'Nearly all the cases involving the civil rights movement were decided on First Amendment grounds.'"

Zuckerberg added, "I don't think it's right for a private

company to censor politicians or the news in a democracy . . . *New York Times v. Sullivan* . . . was actually about an ad with misinformation, supporting Martin Luther King Jr. and criticizing an Alabama police department. The police commissioner sued the *Times* for running the ad, the jury in Alabama found against the *Times,* and the Supreme Court unanimously reversed the decision, creating today's speech standard."

There is much to unpack in those two uninformed paragraphs, but let me begin with this simple observation: free speech—whatever Zuckerberg may believe—did not end slavery in the US. Enslaved people had no right to free speech. They were considered property, with no more power to object to their treatment than did a rug on the floor. And certainly no one, through the exercise of free speech, convinced slaveholders to give up the human beings they insisted they owned. That required the bloodiest quarrel in US history. And when the slaveholding side lost the war, former slave owners continued to treat blacks as if they were property. They clung to slave-era practices for decades as if clinging to life itself.

As for *New York v. Sullivan*, it was about so much more than an "ad with misinformation." First of all, *it contained no misinformation*—certainly not of the sort common in political ads today. What it contained were small mistakes seized on by segregationist politicians in an attempt to intimidate and bankrupt the black ministers (as well as the Yankee press that covered them) who were trying to raise funds for Martin Luther King Jr.'s work.

Let us go back to March 1960. The fledging civil rights movement was fighting for its life when the *New York Times* ran a full-page ad headlined "Heed Their Rising Voices." The ad addressed the plight of black students across the South who were met with "an unprecedented wave" of state terror for trying to exercise their constitutional right to protest and speak out. It claimed some 400 students in Orangeburg, South Carolina, were tear-gassed and attacked with fire hoses for taking part in a protest, and also cited that students at Alabama State College were expelled for singing "My Country, 'Tis of Thee" on the capitol steps. When they tried to reenter the campus, cops armed with shotguns blocked their way. The home of Dr. Martin Luther King Jr. was fire-bombed, which nearly killed his wife and child. "And now they have charged him with 'perjury'—a felony under which they could imprison him for ten years," charged the ad.

In response to the ad, Montgomery's police chief, working in concert with other Alabama officials, sued four black ministers and the *New York Times* for libel. An Alabama jury convicted the defendants, and an Alabama judge awarded a $500,000 judgment, which was a record at the time. Four other Alabama officials, including the governor, also filed lawsuits (demanding between $500,000 and $1 million apiece). Those suits were awaiting trial in 1964 when the Supreme Court decided *New York Times v. Sullivan*.

What misstatements justified the lawsuits and the hefty penalty? Nothing of consequence. As *Newsweek* magazine summed up the errors: "the dining hall was not padlocked, the police did not ring the campus, the students were expelled for another demonstration, and King had been arrested only four times."

In throwing out the lower court's judgment, the Supreme Court threw those four black ministers a lifeline (their personal property, including their cars, had been seized) and immunized the *New York Times* from a white supremacist terror campaign. The court did not rule that lies were okay—as Zuckerberg apparently wants you to believe. It said the public officials could not prevail without showing "actual malice," meaning they had to show that the accused had "knowledge that [the statement] was false" or acted with "reckless disregard of whether it was false or not."

The ad run by the Donald Trump campaign that Zuckerberg was hell-bent on defending did not include any such innocent errors. It repeated conspiracy-theory nonsense and falsely accused former vice president Joseph Biden of promising money to Ukraine if they ended an investigation into a company with ties to Biden's son.

In defense of his decision to run such ads, Zuckerberg is spreading misinformation of his own. He also is libeling the architects of the modern civil rights movement and putting them on a par with lying politicians. It is an insulting, ahistorical defense, as obscene as comparing the Ku Klux Klan to the freedom riders they occasionally lynched.

No wonder Bernice King, Martin Luther King Jr.'s daughter, called out Zuckerberg for his nonsense. "I'd like to help Facebook better understand the challenges #MLK faced from disinformation campaigns launched by politicians," she tweeted. "These campaigns created an atmosphere for his assassination."

The Washington Post, in commenting on Zuckerberg's

speech, noted that Facebook's algorithms already rewarded those willing to make the most outlandish claims: "These mechanics dismantle Mr. Zuckerberg's protestations that his company must remain neutral: Facebook isn't neutral right now. And whichever campaign is most willing to distort—so far this year, it is President Trump's—will most reap the benefits of the site's algorithmic biases."

Facebook's own workers criticized their boss in an open letter signed by more than 250. "We strongly object to this policy as it stands," they wrote. "It doesn't protect voices, but instead allows politicians to weaponize our platform by targeting people who believe that content posted by political figures is trustworthy."

Guardian columnist Simon Jenkins accused Zuckerberg of traveling along the same road as the US Supreme Court, whose 2010 *Citizens United v. Federal Election Commission* decision rewrote the rules of campaign finance, allowing, as Jenkins put it, "lobbyists, corporations, tycoons, anyone with money" to "spend what they liked during an election. It declared open season for fake news, targeted ads and dark money 'Super Pacs'" and "gave us Donald Trump."

Citizens United was only a dramatic development in a long-established trend, one that allowed corporate interests and others with serious money to dominate political dialogue. Not surprisingly, those interests take full advantage of their free speech rights to argue that government is justified in helping to concentrate wealth, in preserving an inequitable status quo, in punishing people for being foreign, colored, and/or poor.

Some 28 percent of respondents to a 2018 survey by The

Democracy Project rated "'big money in politics' as one of their top two issues of concern among 11 possibilities"—putting it in "a statistical tie with 'racism and discrimination.' In addition, a large majority (80 percent) believe that the 'influence of money in politics' is getting worse rather than better." And "over three-quarters (77 percent) agree that 'the laws enacted by our national government these days mostly reflect what powerful special interests and their lobbyists want.'" Only 17 percent believe "the laws enacted by our national government these days mostly reflect what the people want."

It is not coincidental that historically huge disparities in income have occurred at a time when monied interests increasingly control political dialogue and power. Or that, under Trump, we saw a huge tax cut rewarding the wealthy. To the extent political speech shapes our democracy (including voting preferences and policies) and therefore our governance, it can be both cause and casualty of economic inequality.

For all the talk about the impact of money on governance, the situation is only getting worse. In June 2019, the *New York Times* reported that President Trump had raised $24.8 million in twenty-four hours as he launched his reelection campaign. In October, the Associated Press reported that the Trump reelection campaign and the Republican National Committee had raised some $125 million in three months—and that the various Trump-related election entities had raised more than $300 million in the most recent ten months. Such huge amounts of money pouring into political campaigns is something never previously seen.

In early October 2019, *The Washington Post* reported, "At

this point in the last election, Trump's campaign employed 19 consultants. Now, there are more than 200. When Trump had all but locked up the nomination by May 2016, he had spent $63 million. Thus far, pro-Trump committees have spent $531 million."

The unsettling impact of money on politics has long been recognized, which is what led to the Bipartisan Campaign Reform Act of 2002. In changing the rules, the *Citizens United* decision brought a new urgency to the discussion of corporate wealth in politics and government.

The court assumed that "so-called outside groups would not corrupt the political system because they would be legally separated from the candidates," noted Lee Fang in *The Nation*. But as we have seen over the past several years, that legal separation has been more symbolic than real. And although the decision superficially treats unions and corporations equally, the playing field is anything but equal. Union spending is limited by federal laws in a way that corporate spending is not.

The problem, however, is not just that unions are neither as empowered nor as wealthy as big corporations but also that individual citizens have virtually no voice at all. And to make matters worse, they have little assurance the speech inundating them is worth listening to.

The First Amendment guarantee of freedom of speech is rooted in the belief that in a competition of ideas, good ideas generally crowd out bad ideas. It assumes that people are basically rational and skilled in recognizing the better argument when they hear it. And it presupposes that dialogue is dominated by real people with an interest in ideas, not by corporations and wealthy individuals hiding behind PACs and other creations, using trickery, appeals to base prejudice, and outright lies to gather gullible people to their side in the interest of commerce.

Also, our approach to freedom of speech was crafted at a time when no one imagined dialogue would be dominated by the likes of Twitter, Facebook, Snapchat, and other apps that specialize in bursts of short, superficial communication.

Writing in the London-based newspaper *City A.M.*, Professor Nayef Al-Rodhan, director of the Geneva Centre for Security Policy's Geopolitics and Global Futures Programme, wondered whether our brains have caught up with how we now communicate. The instant sharing of information, he noted, is "not driven by rational calculations or critical thinking." Instead, people get excited about something they read—which typically confirms what they already believe—and feel compelled to share it. Upon doing so, through "likes" they get instant external validation, along with a nice hit of dopamine. In that process, facts are largely irrelevant.

"While there are undoubtedly social, and even political, benefits to easily accessible information, issues arise when we consider the sheer volume of this content. We have not yet adjusted to this age of 'information overload,' which exposes our crucial inability to filter fiction from reality," wrote Al-Rodhan.

• • •

Much as many of us admire Louis Brandeis's mind and spirit, the society he envisioned has never existed. Instead, we have created a society in which lying is both endemic and purposeful. We have brought the worst values of advertising into the political sphere and wedded that to long-established tactics of political propaganda, even as our political class has learned to use social media to spread disinformation that propagates at a breathtaking rate. The very idea that political speech would expose and therefore vanquish "falsehood and fallacies" now seems incredibly naïve.

Free speech always had limits. But because of our new technological reality, because of the unexpected weaponization of speech, we are having to consider those limits in a new light. We live in a world where it is far from clear that the answer to bad speech is more speech; and where a foreign power, thanks to our freedom of expression, may well be responsible for the election of a US president. We live in a time when a frightened white minority within the larger white majority fights to maintain control of our country; and when large corporations and cynical functionaries—eager to exploit fear—have a bigger megaphone (including their own television news networks) than anyone speaking for the powerless and dispossessed. We live in an era when the US awarded its presidency to a man who lost the election by roughly three million votes, and who, with the cooperation of a submissive Senate, has appointed judges determined to thwart the will of the public; has proposed policies, supported largely by lies, designed to further divide an already polarized nation; and caters to an irrational mob whose most fanatical elements want to refight the Civil War.

All of this raises a host of difficult questions: If the

Brandeisian view of speech is fatally flawed, what is a better, or at least a more realistic, view? Is it possible to reverse these trends that are destroying our democracy? How do we balance an array of important societal values that compete with the value of free speech? How, in short, do we enable a relatively enlightened majority to rescue our country from an embittered, backward-looking minority? And what happens to speech—which has never been totally free—in the process?

1

LIBERATING THE FIRST AMENDMENT

What is free speech? The meaning might seem obvious: the right to say whatever comes into your mind wherever you happen to be. Yet everybody knows you can't scream fire with impunity in a crowded movie theater or slander people just because they're jerks.

So let's talk about protected speech—speech covered by the First Amendment, which states, "Congress shall make no law respecting an establishment of religion, or prohibiting the free exercise thereof; or abridging the freedom of speech, or of the press; or the right of the people peaceably to assemble, and to petition the Government for a redress of grievances."

The plain meaning is that government cannot tell you what you can or cannot say. There are, of course, exceptions of the sort mentioned above. You can't incite violence, threaten people, exhibit child pornography, or do other things deemed imminently dangerous or blatantly immoral. Otherwise, as far as the government is concerned, you are pretty much free to say, write, or publish whatever pops into your head.

That has not always been true. Even though the First Amendment, along with the rest of the Bill of Rights, was ratified in 1791, it took Congress less than a decade to effectively discard it. The 1798 Alien and Sedition Acts made it a crime—punishable by deportation, fine, or imprisonment—to publish "false, scandalous, [or] malicious writing" against the Federalist government or "to oppose any measure or measures of the government."

Publishers and politicians who dared to criticize Federalists officials were jailed. Congressman Matthew Lyon, a Republican who represented both Vermont and Kentucky, was imprisoned for accusing President John Adams of "ridiculous pomp, foolish adulation, and selfish avarice." Pamphleteer Thomas Cooper was incarcerated for pointing out that, under Adams, the US had taken on new costs, including being "saddled with the expense of a permanent navy and a standing army."

Thomas Jefferson's presidency brought an end to such foolishness, but it brought no respect for the First Amendment itself. That was more than a century away.

Throughout the early part of the nineteenth century, to speak out against slavery in slave-owning states was to risk the loss of both your business and your life. As author Akhil Reed Amar pointed out, "Across the South, mere criticism of slavery became a crime, and the Republican Party was in effect outlawed." The last thing slaveholders wanted to hear were abolitionists urging them to give up their hard-earned (and hardworking) property.

As professor Russel B. Nye observed, "The moment that the South said, in effect, 'You cannot discuss slavery, because slaves are my property and discussion might ultimately destroy the value of that property,' it assumed an untenable and thoroughly dangerous position which very nearly became imposed upon the nation at large."

In much of the South, abolitionist literature was simply destroyed on sight; and the abolitionists themselves did not fare much better. "Although they admitted that freedom of speech was an 'inestimable' privilege," noted historian Susan Wyly-Jones, "the residents of Sandersville, Georgia, . . . considered it perfectly justifiable to suppress publications that encouraged 'the plunder of our property and the murder of our citizens.' The citizens of St. Louis, Missouri, admitted that the First Amendment protected free speech but called that protection merely a 'conventional reservation' that in no way gave the abolitionists the 'moral right' to criticize slavery."

As a result, added Wyly-Jones, countless communities "ordered postmasters to destroy the offending publications and appointed vigilance committees to ferret out any that may have escaped into the community. These committees enjoyed virtually limitless powers as police, prosecution, and jury for those suspected of circulating . . . antislavery pamphlets."

Even in New York City the postmaster "withheld the American Anti-Slavery Society's publications from the mails for a time in 1831," noted Nye. A simple glance at the mailing wrapper was enough to show "the material was incendiary." The problem was so acute that Congress eventually passed legislation mandating that mail be delivered. Nonetheless, Attorney General Caleb Cushing decided in 1857 that the law did not apply to printed matter "the design and tendency of which are to promote insurrections."

In summer 1835, Amos Dresser of Cincinnati was traveling through the South selling the Bible to raise money for college. He arrived in Nashville that July and sent his travel trunk for repairs. He "did not take the precaution to remove from it a number of Anti-Slavery publications that had been used in packing his Bibles in the box," reported the *Anti-Slavery Record*. The literature was discovered and the rumor spread that Dresser intended to "excite the slaves to insurrection." A so-called vigilance committee found him guilty of belonging to the Anti-Slavery Society and sentenced him to twenty lashes with "a heavy cow skin" whip. He was ordered to leave town within twenty-four hours. After the beating, Dresser fled, leaving most of his possessions behind.

Newspaper publishers also were targeted.

In 1933, Elijah Lovejoy began publishing a religiously oriented newspaper in Saint Louis, Missouri, that focused largely on the anti-slavery cause. "Freedom of speech and press," the good citizens informed him, "does not imply a moral right . . . to freely discuss the subject of slavery."

Hostility grew so intense that Lovejoy moved his operation up the road to Alton, Illinois. Three times mobs destroyed his presses. Finally, Alton's city fathers demanded Lovejoy cease publication. Lovejoy replied in writing, invoking his right "to speak and publish my sentiments," which was given him "by my Maker; and is solemnly guaranteed to me by the constitution of the United States and of this state." In November 1837, the mob again came for his presses. Lovejoy was shot and killed trying to protect his property.

In 1845, Cassius M. Clay, publisher of an anti-slavery newspaper called *True American*, was thrown out of what he thought was a public meeting of local notables in the Lexington, Kentucky, courthouse. It turned out that the purpose of the meeting was to formulate a strategy for shutting down Clay's newspaper. A three-man delegation presented him with the demand that he "discontinue the publication of the paper called the 'True American,' as its further continuance, in our judgment, is dangerous to the peace of our community, and to the safety of our homes and families."

The letter accused his paper of "agitating and exciting our community to an extent of which you can scarcely be aware. We do not approach you in the form of a threat; but we owe it to you to state that, in our judgment, your own safety, as well as the repose and peace of the community, are involved in your answer."

Clay shot back that the request was "a base and dishonorable one" and added: "In every case of violence by the blacks since publication of my paper, it has been proven, and will be again proven by my representatives, if my life should fail to be spared, that there have been special causes for their action independent of, and having no relation whatever to the 'True

American' or its doctrines. . . . Go tell your secret conclave of cowardly assassins that C. M. Clay knows his rights and how to defend them."

The town leaders disassembled Clay's press and shipped the pieces to Cincinnati.

Even after slavery was outlawed and the Confederate States were forced to rejoin the Union, the First Amendment went largely unrecognized.

Ida B. Wells, a pioneering black educator and journalist, was co-owner and editor of the *Memphis Free Speech and Headlight.* Her downfall was publishing an editorial in 1892 honoring a friend and seven others who had been lynched. "Eight Negroes lynched since the last issue of the Free Speech, three for killing a white man, and five on the same old racket—the alarm about raping white women. The same program for hanging, then shooting bullets into lifeless bodies," she wrote. "Nobody in this section of the country believes the old threadbare lie that Negro men rape white women. If Southern white men are not careful, they will overreach themselves and public sentiment will have a reaction. A conclusion will then be reached which will be very damaging to the moral reputation of their women."

A mob destroyed Wells's paper and forced her to leave town. No one was held to account.

• • •

"Despite its centrality to our culture today, the First Amendment in the early 20th century was largely a dead letter," observed law professor Thomas Healy. "The Supreme Court had never upheld a free speech claim, and lower courts had approved the censorship of books and films, the prohibition of street-corner speeches and bans on labor protests and profanity."

John Paul Stevens compared the first century of the Bill of Rights to "the Magna Carta—a relatively static symbol expressing the general idea that the federal government has an obligation to obey the law of the land." Only in the second century, he added, did it become "a dynamic force in the development of American law."

A turning point was reached in 1919. World War I was finally over, but civil libertarians were still reeling. During the war, critics of US policy were arrested, deported, and otherwise persecuted. The Bolshevik Revolution had fueled suspicion of foreigners, and the attorney general and other officials advocated brutal suppression of dissidents.

In that atmosphere, the Supreme Court considered the case of five Russian-born US residents who had been convicted under the Sedition Act of 1918. Their crime was printing and distributing pamphlets "intended to bring the form of Government of the United States into contempt, scorn, contumely and disrepute." The 7–2 decision (*Abrams v. United States*), authored by Justice John Hessin Clarke, agreed that "the language of these circulars was obviously intended to provoke and to encourage resistance to the United States in the war."

Oliver Wendell Holmes Jr.—joined by Louis Brandeis—dissented. In the service of that dissent, Holmes wrote a ringing defense of free speech, even for objectionable ideas.

"I think that we should be eternally vigilant against attempts to check the expression of opinions that we loathe and believe to be fraught with death, unless they so imminently threaten immediate interference with the lawful and pressing purposes of the law that an immediate check is required to save the country."

It was to be one of many times that Holmes and Brandeis came together to champion the notion that the best defense against repugnant ideas was better ideas.

Six years later, the Supreme Court considered what was to become a landmark free speech case. This time the court weighed the fate of Benjamin Gitlow, a socialist politician convicted of publishing a "Left Wing Manifesto" in defiance of the New York Criminal Anarchy law. The majority upheld the conviction, reasoning that the state had every right to protect itself against the threat Gitlow's article represented. Again, Holmes and Brandeis dissented, arguing for a less restrictive view of speech.

But even in upholding the conviction, the court made an important concession—that freedom of speech and of the press was protected not only from federal infringement but also from infringement by the states. Those rights were, as Justice Edward Sanford put it, "among the fundamental personal rights and 'liberties' protected by the due process clause of the Fourteenth Amendment from impairment by the States."

That was huge, clearing up, once and for all, any doubt about whether states were also bound by the First Amendment.

The 1927 case of Charlotte Anita Whitney, the Californian

convicted of criminal syndicalism for joining the Communist Party, affirmed the extended reach of the First Amendment. In his famously eloquent concurrence, Brandeis (joined by Holmes) wrote, "Despite arguments to the contrary which had seemed to me persuasive, it is settled that the due process clause of the Fourteenth Amendment applies to matters of substantive law as well as to matters of procedure. Thus all fundamental rights comprised within the term 'liberty' are protected by the Federal Constitution from invasion by the States. The right of free speech, the right to teach, and the right of assembly are, of course, fundamental rights."

• • •

As the United States acknowledged that it had a First Amendment worth honoring, it necessarily had to wrestle with where to draw the line. Exactly how free, in other words, could free speech be?

Part of that answer was provided by Walter Chaplinsky, a Jehovah's Witness in New Hampshire who became angry because a town marshal stood by when onlookers attacked him as he preached. In his anger, Chaplinsky lashed out at the marshal, calling him a "racketeer" and a "damned Fascist." Chaplinsky was arrested and convicted of offensive speech.

In 1942, the Supreme Court came down on the marshal's side. Certain words, reasoned the court, were so infuriating that they had no useful role to play in society. "These include the lewd and obscene, the profane, the libelous, and the insulting or 'fighting' words those which by their very utterance inflict injury or tend to incite an immediate breach of the peace. It has been well observed that such utterances are no essential part of any exposition of ideas, and are of such slight social value as a step to truth that any benefit that may be derived from them is clearly outweighed by the social interest in order and morality."

Over the years, the court has regularly revisited the question of what is acceptable and what is not, what speech merits protection and what speech deserves punishment. In 1968, it looked at draft cards and decided the government was entitled to prohibit burning them to protest the Vietnam War.

In 1989, the court took on flag burning and decided (5–4) it was okay with that. "Could the government . . . prohibit the burning of state flags? Of copies of the Presidential seal? Of the Constitution?" wrote Justice William Brennan for the majority. "In evaluating these choices under the First Amendment, how would we decide which symbols were sufficiently special to warrant this unique status? To do so, we would be forced to consult our own political preferences, and impose them on the citizenry, in the very way that the First Amendment forbids us to do."

In 2003, the court contemplated cross burning, looking at two separate incidents that violated a Virginia law. In one instance, neighbors attempted to burn a cross on a black resident's lawn in Virginia Beach. The other involved a thirty-foot-high cross burned at a KKK rally.

The court rather confusingly ruled that the statute was only partly constitutional. In other words, while anti-cross-burning statutes could be constitutional, the Virginia statute was not constitutional enough—and therefore could not stand. Nonetheless, the court recognized cross burning as a "a particularly virulent form of intimidation" and "of such slight social value as a step to truth that any benefit that may be derived from [it] is clearly outweighed by the social interest in order and morality." Therefore, a properly drawn anti-cross-burning statute would be fine.

So what about neo-Nazis marching through otherwise peaceful areas and shouting scary or vaguely threatening slogans? The courts have consistently found that kind of speech okay—as the decision favoring the Charlottesville rabble-rousers confirmed.

Prior to the Charlottesville tragedy, the most notorious such episode in ACLU history had taken place in 1978, when the ACLU aligned itself with Nazis planning to march through Skokie, a largely Jewish suburb of Chicago, which many Holocaust survivors called home.

That march never took place, largely because the Nazis got cold feet; but the ACLU decision to represent them evoked endless anger and precipitated a membership crisis.

Unlike during the Skokie imbroglio, complaints about Charlottesville came from both within and without the organization. Many critics argued for the ACLU to rethink its policy. When white supremacists were welcome in the White House (including on the senior staff) and proliferating on social media, and hate crimes were on the rise, should defending Nazis be anyone's priority?

At an event arranged by the ACLU, one of the featured speakers, law professor Charles Lawrence, raised a version of that question. He affirmed his belief that the ACLU should not "abandon its bedrock principle that for a century has served us so well." But what if defense of white supremacy "negates my humanity, asserts my non-citizenship, excludes me from democracy's conversation, calls for my extermination, makes possible and then justifies the murder of my son or daughter? . . . Does the injury that it does to me and all people of color make it different than the injury of other offensive or unpopular views?"

He argued for "an open-minded consideration" of his question, which "might lead us to a new way to hold [on to] the bedrock principles of the First Amendment, a way that serves those principles more fully rather than endangering them."

When I spoke to David Goldberger, the Jewish attorney who handled the 1978 Nazi case for the ACLU, he expressed profound disagreement with Lawrence. He found Lawrence's comment's "hurtful because they seemed indifferent to the pain that I and other Jews feel when racists make bigoted public statements about us. We too are capable of feeling pain. The difference, of course, is that the Jews who continued in their support for the ACLU during Skokie and after—and there were many—knew that the pain had to be tolerated because protection of freedom of speech in a democracy was more important."

• • •

The question Lawrence raised cannot simply be dismissed out of hand. Does protecting free speech in any meaningful way necessarily mean protecting the rights of Nazis to chant, "Jews will not defeat us"? Does it necessitate equating pure propaganda with meaningful political speech? Does it require accepting the spread of vicious and virulent misinformation on the internet?

Andrew Marantz, author of *Antisocial: Online Extremists, Techno-Utopians, and the Hijacking of the American Conversation*, pointed out how much has changed from the days "when people associated social media with Barack Obama or the Arab Spring" and Twitter executives saw their company as "the free-speech wing of the free-speech party." He wrote, "No one believes anymore" that the internet is necessarily an engine of progress. "Not after the social-media-fueled campaigns of Narendra Modi and Rodrigo Duterte and Donald Trump; not after the murder of Heather Heyer in Charlottesville, Va.; not after the massacres in a synagogue in Pittsburgh, two mosques in Christchurch, New Zealand, and a Walmart in a majority-Hispanic part of El Paso." To some extent, he pointed out, those tragedies were all gestated deep in the bowels of the very social media that once seemed the key to harmony and understanding.

What is finally clear, Marantz argued (along with Lawrence and others), is that "unchecked speech can expose us to real risks." Some speech, in other words, may be so noxious that it destroys both decency and truth. But what do we do with that insight? Do we aggressively try to root out hate speech? Do we police social media for blatant lies masquerading as truth?

In 2019, as South Africa considered hate speech legislation, Deputy Justice Minister John Jeffery highlighted an attitudinal shift caused by the ubiquity of new media: "Before, people would say things to each other and there would be no record. With social media, there is a record. . . . We do feel the need for there to be consequences."

But the task of sorting out good speech from bad—or hate speech from merely insensitive or provocative language—is challenging. As University of Richmond professor Erik Nielson pointed out, hate "is a dangerously elastic label, one that has long been used in America to demonize unpopular expression. If we become overzealous in our efforts to limit so-called hate speech, we run the risk of setting a trap for the very people we're trying to defend." If we allowed grating voices "to be silenced on grounds that they promote hate, we'd find ourselves scrambling to defend the radical poets, musicians, filmmakers and other artists who have pushed the boundaries of expression into what could arguably amount to hate speech, but who have done so from the vanguard of social and political protest."

"Sometimes when you create these laws, they are used by the powerful to silence the powerless," pointed out Pierre de Vos, a constitutional law expert at the University of Cape Town. "If I say white people are privileged or stole land, that might be hate speech."

Stephen Newman, of York University in Toronto, described a student-painted mural that appeared on campus depicting a young man, holding a stone, wearing a Palestinian flag kerchief, juxtaposed against a bulldozer. "Those who objected to the mural insisted that it was hate speech and demanded that it be taken down," recalled Newman, whereas the mural's defenders "claimed that it was protected political speech and accused those who wanted it removed of seeking to suppress expression supportive of the Palestinian cause. To the mural's defenders the allegation of hate speech was a cynical ploy to silence Israel's critics."

In recent years, the courts have been clogged with cases in which one group believes it has been maligned or harmed by another group exercising what it sees as its right to free speech.

In 2013, the US Court of Appeals for the Ninth Circuit, in California, found itself pondering so-called conversion therapy, a therapeutic practice driven by the conviction that you can literally talk people out of being gay. The legislature, deeming such therapy potentially harmful, banned its use on teens. Lawyer Mat Staver called the ban unnecessarily and "breathtakingly broad." The regulation, argued Staver, had intruded "on protected constitutional liberties of freedom of speech."

The Court of Appeals rejected that argument, deciding unanimously, in August 2013, that the First Amendment "does not prevent a state from regulating treatment even when that treatment is performed through speech alone."

The Pacific Justice Institute (which calls itself a "legal defense organization specializing in the defense of religious freedom, parental rights, and other civil liberties") denounced the decision and proclaimed it "a dark day for those who believe in the 1st Amendment and the rights of parents over the proper upbringing of their children."

In 2014, the US Supreme Court declined without comment to review the decision, allowing it to stand.

Tampa instituted a similar ban, which also was challenged. A magistrate judge who reviewed the statute in February 2019 reached a different decision than the California judges. She said the city had presented no proof that the therapy was harmful and concluded the ban was an unconstitutional prohibition on protected speech. A US district judge upheld the decision, but not on First Amendment grounds. Instead, the judge concluded that regulating such therapy was a function of the state, not of local government.

Comparable disputes have arisen concerning laws aiming to regulate speech around abortion. In June 2018, confronted with a California law mandating crisis pregnancy clinics to give patients information on abortion, a divided (5–4) Supreme Court invalidated the law.

Justice Clarence Thomas, writing for the majority, chafed at the notion that clinics were forced to "provide a government-drafted script about the availability of state sponsored services"—including abortion—"as well as contact information for how to obtain them. . . . By requiring petitioners to inform women how they can obtain state-subsidized abortions—at the same time petitioners try to dissuade women from choosing that option—the licensed notice plainly 'alters the content' of petitioners' speech."

In June 2018, the Supreme Court ruled (7–2) in favor of a Colorado baker who complained that being forced to make a wedding cake for a same-sex couple amounted to "compelled speech." The court declined, however, to decide the case along free speech lines. Instead, in a decision written by Anthony Kennedy, the court concluded that the Colorado Civil Rights

Commission had not given the baker a fair hearing and that its finding of discrimination was therefore "inconsistent with the 1st Amendment's guarantee that our laws be applied in a manner that is neutral toward religion."

A year later, in September 2019, the Arizona Supreme Court ruled that a Phoenix antidiscrimination ordinance did not obligate artists to create custom wedding invitations for gay couples. The ruling acknowledged that the complaining artists' beliefs "may seem old-fashioned, or even offensive to some. But the guarantees of free speech and freedom of religion are not only for those who are deemed sufficiently enlightened, advanced, or progressive. They are for everyone."

For the foreseeable future, we no doubt will see such legal challenges continue, as American society wrestles with the question of where to draw the lines when free speech is involved.

john a. powell (he prefers not to capitalize his name), a law professor at UC Berkeley and a former legal director of the ACLU, argues for a broad perspective—one in which speech is considered only in conjunction with other social goals and rights.

He has compared the right to speech to the right to drive a car. "I don't have a right to pollute; but I might [if society] weighed all the pluses and minuses, all the benefits and burdens, and we decided we're going to allow it. But society could come back and say we've reconsidered and we're not going to allow it. And I can't then say I have a right to drive a gasoline combustible car. So what I basically say is a lot of stuff that's being talked about through the concept of free speech is actually social rights. . . . When you consider it, you consider the full [scope] of how it affects people."

His larger point is that few rights, including the right to speech, are valued in isolation. Most rights are valued in a broad context, often in the "service of something else." So if you divorce speech from "encouraging the exchange of ideas," what are we really encouraging? Are we saying, "We're not going to protect anyone from cyberbullying because we have this sacred cow called speech"?

"In the sixties with the free speech movement," powell said, "we were pushing the envelope. We were thinking about the restructuring of society in a way to bring other people in, bring other voices in." He added, "I represented the Klan. I do believe in free speech. But I'm not slavish to free speech. What does free speech mean in the age of artificial intelligence? [ACLU co-founder and first executive director] Roger Baldwin didn't tell us that. What does free speech mean in the age of trolling and Russia corrupting our . . . news? Roger Baldwin didn't tell us that. So again, free speech was always in service to something, and now it's actually being used as a weapon against people and against institutions. And I don't think we should be sanguine with that."

Raymond J. de Souza, a Catholic priest and columnist for the *National Post* of Canada, made a similar argument as he struggled with the implications of free speech in the aftermath of the *Charlie Hebdo* mass murder in France—a massacre triggered by the publication's decision to publish cartoons that mocked the prophet Muhammad. "The key question raised by the *Charlie Hebdo* aftermath," wrote De

Souza, "is whether free speech is part of a deeper conception of liberty and the common good—and therefore we defend its abuses—or contrariwise, it is only the mere indulgence of 'expressive individualism.' . . . In which case, why bother?"

In short, what is the purpose of free speech—and at what price, and with what limits, do we protect it? "To argue for free speech untethered from virtue," concluded De Souza, "is akin to insisting that supporting the constabulary includes defending police beatings."

2

THE ROOT OF ALL EVIL

The music is unmistakable, the beat irresistible—the assertive sound of 1970s funk. It begins with the bass guitar, then *boom*, the percussion, and finally the O'Jays, in unison and in harmony, chant, "Money, money, money, money . . . money."

On screen appear skyscrapers, a private jet, and words that gradually form a sentence: "What if you could make [a huge check flashes on the screen] a difference?"

Then the man himself strolls into view, resplendent in a long, dark coat, dark suit, and blue patterned tie, strutting in a way that makes undeniably clear he is master of all: the king at whose feet the famous come to learn. The focus briefly shifts to his three adult children, and finally to the celebrity contestants. Meanwhile, the O'Jays continue to sing.

The mini movie unfolds in roughly a minute. But it is one

of the more brilliant minutes in television; and it burns into our mind an indelible image of success at an unimaginable level, an image that became the public persona of Donald Trump and, ultimately, launched a presidency.

Donald Trump was certainly not the first wealthy person to decide that wealth entitled him to rule the world. But he perfectly embodied the ethos, in style and substance, that, decency be damned, everything—everyone—is for sale.

• • •

In the United States' new gilded age, in which big money has become the addictive yet poisonous fuel on which modern politics runs, and when democracy itself often seems for sale, some thoughtful souls see a possible salvation in campaign spending reform. Many of them worshipped at the altar of McCain-Feingold, a bill proposed in 2001 that they hoped would ease dependence on the money increasingly corroding the democratic dream.

The *Sarasota Herald-Tribune* was one of many publications arguing the case: "The flood of money in politics has seriously undermined the public's faith in government and probably plays a large role in the ever-dwindling voter turnout. . . . This bill won't cure all the ills of the political process, but it's a start. It offers reasonable restrictions that would reduce the likelihood that elected officials base their decisions on who has stuffed their campaign treasuries."

Bernice Powell Jackson, a syndicated columnist for the

black press, noted that 90 percent of House and Senate races were won by the candidate with the most money, making campaign finance reform "not only a voting rights issue, but a civil rights issue" for the poor who were "being priced out of our democracy."

Even local politics seemed to be dominated by money. "When it takes $2 million to mount a campaign in Maine, that's got to tell you something. Something is amiss," a local businessman told the *Maine Sunday Telegram*.

The McCain-Feingold Act, passed in March 2002, was supposed to change that—or at least be a step in that direction. The measure, also known as the Bipartisan Campaign Reform Act of 2002, or BCRA, was an outgrowth of a series of scandals and abuses, beginning with Watergate. It aimed at dramatically reducing the role of money in politics by placing specific limits on money raised by national political parties and by barring the running of ads targeting any specific federal candidate within thirty days of a primary or caucus and within sixty days of a general election. It also prohibited corporations, unions, and other independent entities from running such ads.

President George W. Bush, who had opposed portions of the legislation, nonetheless signed it. "I think it improves the system," he said, later telling reporters, "I wouldn't have signed it if I was really unhappy with it."

Senate minority whip Mitch McConnell, joined by the National Rifle Association, the AFL-CIO, and others, immediately filed suit against the legislation. "Not since the Alien and Sedition Acts, enacted in the earliest days of our Republic, could criminal sanctions be so easily incurred simply by engaging in such core political speech," said their complaint.

In December 2003, the Supreme Court, in a long, convoluted, and sharply divided (5–4) opinion, upheld key provisions of the law. It upheld the restrictions on ads released within weeks of elections and agreed it was fine for government to limit so-called soft money contributions to political parties. It struck down a provision barring political contributions from people too young to vote and abolished limits on political spending by corporations and others who were independent of a political candidate.

That decision favoring independent expenditures was an acknowledgment of a 1976 Supreme Court decision (*Buckley v. Valeo*) that distinguished "contributions" from "expenditures." Free speech, in the estimation of the court, was not significantly infringed upon by limiting contributions but was infringed upon if the government limited one's independent expenditures, which was considered a more direct attack on freedom of speech.

As Yale University law professor Heather Gerken put it, "The snake in this garden of campaign-finance Eden was the Supreme Court's decision in *Buckley v. Valeo*. . . . By lifting the cap on expenditures while leaving in place the cap on contributions, the Supreme Court created a world in which politicians' appetite for money would be limitless, but their ability to get it would not. . . . Political interests inevitably looked for loopholes, they inevitably found loopholes, and they inevitably drove big trucks of money through those loopholes."

Even at the time, some observers thought the court's reasoning was problematic—if not outright bizarre. "The biggest beneficiaries," predicted the *New York Daily News*, "will be candidates with broad-based backing . . . along with presidential and congressional hopefuls with substantial personal or family fortune, who are now free to spend as much of their own money as they want."

"I will find a way to spend my money—and so will Joe Coors," General Motors heir Steward Mott told the *Daily News*.

Nevertheless, Senator John McCain, a prime mover of the 2002 legislation, counted the 2003 (*McConnell v. Federal Election Commission*) ruling as a victory. "Now, no politician can pick up the phone, call the head of a major corporation and say, 'Give me a million dollars,'" he told reporters.

• • •

Those earlier decisions provided an important context for *Citizens United v. Federal Election Commission*, the controversial Supreme Court decision that ripped the heart out of the McCain-Feingold Act.

The *Christian Science Monitor*'s report on the 2010 decision recalled the 2003 decision by "a different lineup of justices" that had come to a very different set of conclusions. *The Wall Street Journal* similarly noted the political shift in the court's thinking: "A deeply divided Supreme Court struck down limits on corporate political spending, overturning two precedents and underscoring the impact of former president George W. Bush's appointments to the court." Those appointees, John Roberts and Samuel Alito, were part of the 5–4 majority that blocked the government from restricting spending by corporations and unions on political campaigns.

In the majority opinion, authored by Justice Anthony Kennedy, the court stated, "By suppressing the speech of manifold corporations, both for-profit and nonprofit, the Government prevents their voices and viewpoints from reaching the public and advising voters on which persons or entities are hostile to their interests."

The remedy, concluded the majority, was to allow corporations to spend whatever they wished on political ads, even if an election was imminent. "Government may not suppress political speech on the basis of the speaker's corporate identity," declared Justice Kennedy's opinion, which extended First Amendment privileges enjoyed by humans to corporations.

Senate judiciary chair Patrick Leahy observed the decision was "likely to change the course of our democracy and could threaten the public's confidence in the Court's impartiality." Anna Burger, secretary-treasurer of the Service Employees International Union, worried that "unlimited corporate spending" was likely to "drown out the voices" of the voters and candidates who "should really be at the center of the political process."

Even President Barack Obama was critical. In his January 27, 2010, State of the Union message, he said, "Last week, the Supreme Court reversed a century of law to open the floodgates for special interests—including foreign corporations—to spend without limit in our elections. Well, I don't think American elections should be bankrolled by America's most powerful interests, or worse, by foreign entities." In his weekly address, the president said that the ruling "strikes at democracy itself," undermining the republic by elevating the voices of "powerful interests that already drown out the voices of everyday Americans."

The most biting, and certainly the most detailed, criticism came from within the court itself, in the form of Justice John Paul Stevens's dissent, which said the ruling "threatens to undermine the integrity of elected institutions across the nation" and damage the court's credibility. He charged the majority with bending the case to their own agenda: "Essentially, five Justices were unhappy with the limited nature of the case before us, so they changed the case to give themselves an opportunity to change the law." Stevens, in an opinion joined by Ruth Bader Ginsburg, Stephen Breyer, and Sonia Sotomayor, wrote, "For these five Justices to reach their broad ruling, they overturned precedent, as well as the statute."

Stevens thought the idea that corporations, for the purpose of speech, were analogous to sentient, breathing human beings, was absurd: "The basic premise underlying the Court's ruling is its iteration, and constant reiteration, of the proposition that the First Amendment bars regulatory distinctions based on a speaker's identity, including its 'identity' as a corporation. While that glittering generality has rhetorical appeal, it is not a correct statement of the law." Stevens acknowledged that corporations "make enormous contributions to our society" but pointed out that they "are not actually members of it. They cannot vote or run for office. Because they may be managed and controlled by nonresidents, their interests may conflict in fundamental respects with the interests of eligible voters."

Stevens also accused the majority of taking power away from political parties and handing it to self-interested corporations. "Going forward, corporations and unions will be free to spend as much general treasury money as they wish on ads that support or attack specific candidates, whereas national parties will not be able to spend a dime of soft money on ads of any kind. The Court's ruling thus dramatically enhances the role of corporations and unions—and the narrow interests they represent."

In a sarcastic aside, Stevens played out the logical ramifications of the majority's assumption that the "identity" of a speaker was irrelevant: "Such an assumption would have accorded the propaganda broadcasts to our troops by 'Tokyo Rose' during World War II the same protection as speech by Allied commanders. More pertinently, it would appear to afford the same protection to multinational corporations controlled by foreigners as to individual Americans. . . . Under the majority's view, I suppose it may be a First Amendment problem that corporations are not permitted to vote, given that voting is, among other things, a form of speech."

Stevens caustically attacked the idea that, in elevating the role of corporations, the majority was somehow reflecting the values of the Founders. "Those few corporations that existed at the founding were authorized by grant of a special legislative charter. Corporate sponsors would petition the legislature, and the legislature, if amenable, would issue a charter that specified the corporation's powers and purposes and 'authoritatively fixed the scope and content of corporate organization,' including 'the internal structure of the corporation.'"

The Founding Fathers, he added, "[unlike] our colleagues . . . had little trouble distinguishing corporations from human beings, and when they constitutionalized the right to free speech in the First Amendment, it was the free speech of individual Americans that they had in mind." There was no evidence, he added, "to support the notion that the Framers would have wanted corporations to have the same rights as natural persons in the electoral context; we have ample evidence to suggest that they would have been appalled by the evidence of corruption that Congress unearthed in developing BCRA and that the Court today discounts to irrelevance."

Stevens conjectured that giving corporations an unlimited license for political spending might even harm corporations themselves, by forcing them to "use their shareholders' money both to maintain access to, and to avoid retribution from, elected officials. . . . It can impose a kind of implicit tax."

Ultimately, argued Stevens, the majority's position was an unmerited rejection "of the common sense of the American people, who have recognized a need to prevent corporations from undermining self-government since the founding, and who have fought against the distinctive corrupting potential of corporate electioneering since the days of Theodore Roosevelt. It is a strange time to repudiate that common sense. While American democracy is imperfect, few outside the majority of this Court would have thought its flaws included a dearth of corporate money in politics."

• • •

Law professor john powell, an admirer of Stevens's dissent, sees the *Citizens United* ruling as an example of the court doing precisely the opposite of what it claimed to be doing. In his view, instead of protecting speech, the court was disempowering citizens: "The whole idea of having a Bill of Rights was to protect people from the state. Protect people from the consolidation of power. And that's what corporations are, a consolidation of power. . . . When you have courts that protect corporate rights, they actually eviscerate individual rights."

Many aspects of *Citizens United* were extremely unpopular, but the public was not of one mind.

Immediately after the decision, Gallup sent its pollsters into the field and found that 57 percent agreed that campaign donations were a protected form of free speech. "At the same time," reported Gallup, "the majority think it is more important to limit campaign donations than to protect this free-speech right." Some 61 percent of Americans told Gallup that government should be able to put limits on campaign contributions, and 76 percent said government should be able to "limit the amount corporations of unions can give."

In 2013, when Gallup polled opinion on campaign spending limits, it found that 79 percent of Americans were in favor of spending limits for congressional candidates. In that same poll, fully half of respondents said they would vote for a law in which "federal campaigns are funded by the government and all contributions from individuals and private groups are banned."

In short, Americans are happy to concede that people—or corporations—have a right to spend money on political campaigns. But they also believe in limits, that enough is enough—and if the price of getting money out of politics is an infringement on corporate speech, then they are fine with that.

And it's not just radicals and socialists who are disturbed by what they see. As Peggy Noonan, a Republican commentator for *The Wall Street Journal*, put it, "Citizens United gave the rich too much sway in the GOP. The party was better off when it relied on Main Street. It meant they had to talk to Main Street."

In 2018, during an interview with Justice Ruth Bader Ginsburg, I asked her what she considered to be the biggest dangers to democracy today. The first thing she named was "money"—meaning the flood of money into politics—and the second was gerrymandering. She added, "Some of my colleagues will say, as long as the source is disclosed, it's fine. . . . But now there is all that dark money going in."

When rich people's votes mean so much more than those of poor people, when money from corporations gives CEOs the kind of access and influence that no ordinary person could ever dream of having, the very legitimacy of democracy is seriously undermined.

In her research, Anne Baker, a professor of politics at Santa Clara University, has explored the impact of outside contributions—meaning contributions by people who are not constituents—on representation of people who live in congressional districts. She discovered that dependency on outside contributions makes politicians less responsive to their own constituents and encourages "ideological extremity." Irrespective of political party, concluded Baker, "members' dependency on outside contributions draws them in a more extremely liberal or extremely conservative ideological direction."

Baker also noted an outsize responsiveness to wealthy donors at the expense of people who have only a vote to offer. Other research has found the views of lower-income voters have less influence "even on issues that disproportionately affect the quality of their lives."

None of this is surprising. It just confirms common sense—people or institutions willing to donate millions to support political candidates are generally doing it because they want something; and the politicians who depend on them for money are happy to give them what they want.

In changing the rules with its *Citizens United* decision, the Supreme Court brought a new urgency to the discussion of corporate wealth in politics and government.

The court assumed that if outside groups were not formally connected to a candidate, their contributions would not corrupt the political system. That was a fantasy.

Despite the rules against coordination, "parties still exercise a great deal of control over independent spending," observed Professor Gerken. The so-called "independent Super PACs . . . are intimately interconnected with the real parties. . . . The same deep connections run between the Super PACs and the candidates they support. Most of the Super PACs are run by the people who used to run candidates' campaigns."

And although the Supreme Court decision superficially treats unions and corporations equally, the playing field is anything but equal. As Harvard Law School professor Benjamin Sachs has pointed out, "federal law prohibits a union from spending its general treasury funds on politics if individual employees object to such use," whereas "corporations are free to spend their general treasuries on politics even if individual shareholders object."

Campaign spending by corporations vastly outpaces spending by labor. "However this data is sliced, business interests dominate," observed Sheila Krumholz, executive director of the Center for Responsive Politics.

The hijacking of so much of political dialogue by the moneyed class obviously bothers many Americans. But "what do we do when the U.S. Supreme Court . . . claims that we are constitutionally obligated to drown our elections in big money?" asked Bill Nemitz, writer for the *Portland Press Herald* in Maine.

Nemitz's question was a setup for a profile of Jeff Clements, president of American Promise, a group working for a constitutional amendment that would reverse the Supreme Court ruling. Legislators in both houses of Congress have introduced Democracy for All amendments to overturn *Citizens United*. The amendments would re-empower Congress to limit corporate contributions and to establish campaign finance rules.

Speaking on behalf of one such measure in 2019, Senator

Benjamin Cardin, a co-sponsor, declared, "We can't let dark money drown out the voices of everyday Americans. The power of our democracy belongs to the people—not corporations, not the wealthy elite." Congressman Adam Schiff explained, "Amending the Constitution is an extraordinary step, but it is the only way to safeguard our democratic process against the threat of unrestrained and anonymous spending by wealthy individuals and corporations."

In June 2019, New Hampshire became the twentieth state to pass a nonbinding resolution supporting such an amendment. But the road to enactment is anything but clear—as passing a constitutional amendment requires approval by a two-thirds vote in both houses of Congress and ratification by thirty-eight states.

What is clear is that Americans are deeply unhappy with what our leaders have created: a system in which an ordinary person's vote is worth significantly less than that of someone who pays politicians to make time for his or her concerns. It may have been fun watching Trump play a scheming billionaire on a television show, but it is much less fun watching billionaires—or corporations that reflect their values—hijack our democracy.

The inevitable question, of course, is "How do we rescue our democracy?" The answer, alas, is a lot more complicated than just reducing the corrosive influence of dark money.

3

WHAT YOU'RE SEEING IS NOT WHAT'S HAPPENING

In *Post-Truth*, his book-length rumination on the counter-factual world, philosopher Lee McIntyre pointed to a notable milestone reached in November 2016, when the Oxford Dictionaries named "post-truth" its international word of the year. "After seeing a 2,000 percent spike in usage over 2015," McIntyre wrote, "the choice seemed obvious. . . . As a catch-all phrase, 'post-truth' seemed to capture the times. Given the obfuscation of facts, abandonment of evidential standards in reasoning, and outright lying that marked 2016's Brexit vote and the US presidential election, many were aghast. If Donald Trump could claim—without evidence—that if he lost the election it would be because it was rigged against him, did facts and truth even matter anymore?"

"'Post-truth,'" noted the *New York Times*, had vanquished

"a politically charged field that included 'adulting,' 'alt-right,' 'Brexiteer,' 'glass cliff' and 'woke.'" Quoting Katherine Connor Martin, Oxford's head of US dictionaries, the *Times* explained, "The term, whose first known usage in this particular sense was in a 1992 essay in *The Nation* magazine citing the Iran-Contra scandal and the Persian Gulf War, does not represent an entirely new concept. But it does, Ms. Martin said, reflect a step past 'truthiness,' the Stephen Colbert coinage. . . . 'Truthiness is a humorous way of discussing a quality of specific claims,' she said. 'Post-truth is an adjective that is describing a much bigger thing. It's saying that the truth is being regarded as mostly irrelevant.'"

The Washington Post greeted the news with "It's official: Truth is dead. Facts are passé." And the *Christian Science Monitor* conjectured that "the term 'post-truth' may ultimately point to a fundamental shift in how objective truth is interpreted in the 21st century. With the collective knowledge of human civilization at our fingertips through the internet, information is no longer the purview of an intellectual elite. . . . With this democratization of information, however, comes the problem of an oversaturation of information by anyone with an opinion on the facts to the point where it becomes harder to determine what is true and what is merely the product of someone's political agenda."

In July 2018, at a speech before a veterans' group in Kansas City, Donald Trump said something amazing even for him. "Stick with us. Don't believe the crap you see from these people, the fake news. . . . What you're seeing and what you're reading is not what's happening."

The outburst struck CNN politics reporter and editor-at-large Chris Cillizza as "an absolutely remarkable thing for any elected leader to say—especially when that leader is the most powerful person in the country. . . . What Trump is saying is this: I (and those who support me) are the only ones telling you the truth. Anything you hear from anyone who is not me is not to be believed."

The anti-truth imperative, of course, did not begin with Donald Trump. Trump just made it impossible to avoid acknowledging that much of society was embracing a truly bizarre concept of reality.

In a sense, we have been dealing with the issue of truth in public speech since the beginnings of the republic. Indeed, as noted previously, the Founders explicitly exempted members of Congress from consequences for any words—including false or libelous words—uttered in Congress.

But we have never dealt with a commander in chief who lies as constantly, as transparently, and as shamelessly as Donald Trump, whose many misstatements in 2015 were collectively awarded Lie of the Year by PolitiFact (a Pulitzer Prize–winning fact-checking website). "In considering our annual Lie of the Year, we found our only real contenders were Trump's—his various statements also led our Readers' Poll. But it was hard to single one out from the others. So we have rolled them into one big trophy," announced the website, which listed a number of his whoppers: that 81 percent of whites murdered were killed by blacks (in fact 82 percent were killed by other whites); that thousands of people cheered in New Jersey when the World Trade Center was destroyed on 9/11; that the Mexican government was shipping "the bad ones" to the US. "So far, we've fact-checked more than 70 Trump statements and rated fully three-quarters of them as Mostly False, False, or Pants on Fire," wrote PolitiFact editor Angie Drobnic Holan in a *New York Times* op-ed.

Back in 1952, when anti-Communist zealot and chronic liar Joseph McCarthy was riding high, Hornell Hart, a Duke University sociologist, subjected McCarthy's statements to fact-checking. McCarthy, of course, was notorious for falsely labeling people as Communist at a time when relations between the US and the Soviet Union were tense—and such allegations could get you fired, or worse.

Hart exhaustively investigated fifty specific charges McCarthy had made and found that none had merit. For all his bluster, McCarthy had not identified a single hidden Communist who had infiltrated a US institution.

Nonetheless, the media continued to shower McCarthy with attention, and for two more years, until the Senate finally censured him, much of the press gave him the publicity—and credibility—he craved.

One notable exception was Palmer Hoyt, editor and publisher of *The Denver Post*, who announced in February 1953 that he was adopting a special McCarthy policy. Henceforth, declared Hoyt, the *Post* would fact-check McCarthy's allegations and also would give any person accused by McCarthy the opportunity to respond.

Hoyt went on a personal anti-McCarthy crusade. In July 1953, he warned the Harvard Conference on Public Unrest in Education that McCarthy was "usurping the functions of the executive, of the legislative, and of the judicial" branches of government. He added, "Far too many of our national leaders are afraid of Joseph R. McCarthy," and he pointedly included newspaper editors on the list. In 1954, speaking at the Arizona Press Club, he bemoaned "the fifth year of the McCarthy siege against the American mind" and charged McCarthy with making "a shambles of the United States Senate and the American press."

For the most part, Hoyt's journalistic colleagues were not so bold. After *New York Post* editor James Wechsler was called before McCarthy's Senate Permanent Subcommittee on Investigations in apparent retaliation for the *Post* running articles critical of McCarthy, Wechsler demanded that the transcript of his interrogation be released. McCarthy finally did so, in exchange for Wechsler compiling a list of individuals who were fellow members of the Young Communist League to which Wechsler had briefly belonged as a young man. Wechsler submitted the transcript—largely a browbeating by McCarthy—to the American Society of Newspaper Editors, which he hoped would investigate McCarthy for violating freedom of the press.

The editors appointed an eleven-man committee, which could not agree on whether McCarthy had acted improperly. Instead, in August 1953, the group issued a report acknowledging that some committee members "were disturbed by the tenor of the investigation, but do not feel that this single interchange constitutes a clear and present danger to freedom of the press." Four committee members issued a separate report calling McCarthy "a peril to American freedom." The strongest statement the editors could all agree on was "Since the committee is not in agreement . . . it is the responsibility of every editor to . . . decide for himself." Emboldened by what he took to be his exoneration, McCarthy immediately called upon those members who had declined to condemn him to investigate *The Washington Post* for coverage he deemed unfair and unduly critical. "I am sure you will agree with me," wrote McCarthy, "that when a newspaper is used for the purpose of deceiving the public—then freedom of the press is thereby gravely endangered." He also asked those editors to "correct" the work of their colleagues who had pronounced him "a peril."

Senator McCarthy's many similarities to President Trump are impossible to ignore: his tendency to distort the truth, his animosity to a critical press, his doubling down on lies, his insistence on seeing exoneration where none exists. But there are also critical differences, including the range of things that Trump lies about, and the power of the presidency, which—even if he did not have a news network and Twitter to back him—dwarfs that of a junior senator from Wisconsin. And while McCarthy was driven, on some level, by anti-Communist ideology, Trump lacks a coherent ideology or intellectual interest; Trump seems driven by vanity, bigotry, personal grievance, and an unshakable belief that he is America and that America must be first. When Trump targets an issue or a person for attack, there is something both merciless and primitive about it, reminiscent of the Incredible Hulk declaring, "Hulk smash!" as his outsize fist lands on a hapless target.

Whereas McCarthy's lies fueled paranoia, Trump's wreak

havoc domestically and internationally—and even have the power to kill. The reality was brought home by his handling of the 2019 coronavirus crisis, which he initially seemed intent on talking away. He promised, repeatedly and falsely, that the arrival of a COVID-19 vaccine was imminent; he suggested the virus was no more worrisome than a seasonal flu; he shared his "hunch" that the experts were wrong about the disease's seriousness; he insisted, wrongly, that tests were easily available for those who wanted them; and he claimed that the virus was going to "disappear . . . like a miracle." He also blamed the United States' testing snafus on Barack Obama. And he accused Democrats of trying to use the virus as a vehicle for impeachment—and therefore of perpetrating a "new hoax."

Having had some experience with Trump's unreliable messaging, the financial markets were not exactly trusting. The day after Trump delivered a televised address intended to calm the markets and the nation, the Dow Jones posted its largest one-day drop ever, leading Lawrence Summers, former treasury secretary and former Harvard University president, to tweet that Trump had set off "what I believe is a new world record for presidential market value destruction."

As *New Yorker* writer Susan Glasser observed, "Trump has spent years devaluing and diminishing facts, experts, institutions, and science—the very things upon which we must rely in a crisis—and his default setting during the coronavirus outbreak has been to deny, delay, deflect, and diminish."

That practice apparently has not much hurt his credibility with his base. A poll by Axios shortly before Trump's televised address found some 62 percent of Republicans, compared to 31 percent of Democrats, agreed with Trump's repeated message that journalists were exaggerating the seriousness of the virus. Republicans also were more likely to doubt the virus could be easily spread. A survey by the Pew Research Center in 2019 similarly found radically different views on facts, depending on political affiliation. Indeed, most respondents from both parties (77 percent of Republicans and 72 percent of Democrats) agreed that Americans from different parties could not even concur on "basic facts."

That Republicans and Democrats see things differently is hardly remarkable, but as Pew noted, the partisanship gap, which rose to record levels during Obama's presidency, has grown even wider under Trump. That reflects not just the growing ugliness in US politics generally, along with the evolution of increasingly polarized broadcast and online media, but also the impact of Trump's war on traditional media and on truth itself.

Ironically, the mainstream press, so often the target of Trump's ire, was instrumental to his rise.

• • •

Prior to the 2016 presidential campaign, CNN had been suffering financially and lacked a clear and feasible mission, reported the *New York Times Magazine* in 2017. "But then along came a presidential candidate who was a human breaking-news event. Trump provided drama and conflict every time he opened his mouth. So too did his growing band of surrogates, who were paid by either the campaign or the network, and in one case both, to defend his statements. Indeed, it often seemed disconcertingly as though Trump had built his entire campaign around nothing so much as his singular ability to fill cable news's endless demand for engaging content. . . . Had Trump lost the election, CNN would probably have returned to its previously scheduled struggle for survival. Instead, it has become more central to the national conversation than at any point in the network's history since the first gulf war." CNN, concluded the *Times*, "helped turn Trump into the Republican front-runner at a time when few others took his candidacy seriously."

CNN had plenty of company in pursuing profit through Trump. As CBS chairman Leslie Moonves famously told the *Hollywood Reporter* in 2016, the Trump phenomenon "may not be good for America, but it's damn good for CBS. . . . Man, who would have expected the ride we're all having right now? . . . The money's rolling in and this is fun. . . . It's a terrible thing to say. But, bring it on, Donald. Keep going."

Moonves later said he had been joking. But he clearly had spoken the truth. As Michelle Amazeen, an assistant communications professor at Rider University, pointed out, "Since the U.S. news media is based on the commercial model—and more eyeballs on the page or the screen is good for business—the networks love it when someone like Donald Trump says outrageous stuff."

In December 2017, researchers Duncan Watts and David Rothschild published a damning indictment of the news media's response to the challenges of covering Trump. The

Columbia Journalism Review article sifted through an array of coverage statistics and found the media to be overwhelmingly—if unwittingly—in Trump's pocket.

"In just six days," reported Watts and Rothschild, "the *New York Times* ran as many cover stories about Hillary Clinton's emails as they did about all policy issues combined in the 69 days leading up to the election." In a review of reporting by mainstream news organizations, they found that reporting on "various Clinton-related email scandals . . . accounted for more sentences than all of Trump's scandals combined (65,000 vs. 40,000) and more than twice as many as were devoted to all of her policy positions."

Watts and Rothschild concluded, "To the extent that voters mistrusted Hillary Clinton, or considered her conduct as secretary of state to have been negligent or even potentially criminal, or were generally unaware of what her policies contained or how they may have differed from Donald Trump's, these numbers suggest their views were influenced more by mainstream news sources than by fake news. . . . Without discounting the role played by malicious Russian hackers and naïve tech executives, we believe that fixing the information ecosystem is at least as much about improving the real news as it about stopping the fake stuff."

Conventional media also tied itself into knots by striving, in an attempt at fairness, to cast the candidates' respective sins in the same harsh light. The result was articles such as one that ran on *Politico* in 2016, which asked, "Are Clinton and Trump the Biggest Liars Ever to Run for President?"

The answer: "In their personalities and their politics,

Hillary Clinton and Donald Trump might not have much in common, but in the public eye they share one glaring characteristic: A lot of people don't believe what they say.... Clinton isn't an egregious fabricator like Trump, but she's been dogged her whole career by a sense of inauthenticity—the perception that she's selling herself as something she isn't, whether that's a feminist, a liberal, a moderate or a fighter for the working class." *Politico*, in short, equated Clinton's supposed insincerity (which is an impossible thing to accurately assess) with Trump's blatant and unrelenting lies.

One consequence of the media's—and particularly TV's—attempt to promote fairness or balance is that chronic liars and con artists have found themselves elevated to the level of thoughtful public figures.

As *New York Times* columnist Michelle Goldberg reminded her readers, "Journalists, perhaps seeking to appear balanced, have sometimes described Trump's claims about Biden as 'unsubstantiated' or 'unsupported.' That is misleading, because it suggests more muddiness in the factual record than actually exists. Trump isn't making unproven charges against Biden. He is blatantly lying about him. He and his defenders are spreading a conspiracy theory that is the precise opposite of the truth."

Corey Lewandowski, a former Trump operative (who for a while snagged a paying commentator's slot on CNN), is a vivid example of the folly of the quest for false journalistic balance. Pressed by counsel to the House Judiciary Committee to account for a false assertion made during an interview on MSNBC, Lewandowski shot back, "I have no obligation to be honest to the media because they're just as dishonest as anybody else."

Trump did not create this fact-free, determinedly dishonest approach to public dialogue and governance. He is as much its product as its instigator. But he also is its most prominent practitioner, and he has taken that practice to unprecedented heights.

He dismissed his own government's *Fourth National Climate Assessment* and its warnings that action must be "taken to reduce greenhouse gas emissions and to adapt to the changes that will occur" with a dismissive "Next time we will have better scenarios." Months later, he drove home his point by responding to Amy Klobuchar's snow-accompanied announcement of her candidacy for the presidency with "Well, it happened again. Amy Klobuchar announced that she is running for President, talking proudly of fighting global warming while standing in a virtual blizzard of snow, ice and freezing temperatures. Bad timing."

He instigated a bizarre episode in fall 2019 in which his erroneous tweet about Hurricane Dorian led to pressure on the National Oceanic and Atmospheric Administration to make its forecast conform to his twisted facts.

He instigated an impeachment inquiry by attempting to force Ukraine to commit to finding evidence for a wacky conspiracy theory that defied all common sense—and flew directly in the face of facts that the US intelligence community had provided. And he consistently, as already noted, misrepresented the truth about the 2019 coronavirus.

There is an obvious reluctance in many quarters to call

out the president's chronic lying for what it is. That's understandable, if regrettable, when it comes to civil servants who work for him or politicians who believe he can destroy their careers. But it also affects certain news providers—who share the inclination of *Denver Post* publisher Palmer Hoyt's contemporaries who bent themselves into pretzels to give Joseph McCarthy the deeply unmerited benefit of the doubt.

In early 2017, *Wall Street Journal* editor-in-chief Gerard Baker found himself hard-pressed to defend his decision to refer to the Trump administration's false statements as something other than lies. "I'd be careful about using the word 'lie.' 'Lie' implies much more than just saying something that's false. It implies a deliberate intent to mislead," insisted Baker on *Meet the Press*.

In an article in *The Wall Street Journal*, he defended his policy: "Note that I said I'd be 'careful' in using the word 'lie.' I didn't ban the word from the *Journal*'s lexicon. . . . [It's] not because I don't believe that Trump has said things that are untrue. Nor is it because I believe that when he says things that are untrue we should refrain from pointing it out. This is exactly what the *Journal* has done. . . . I believe the right approach is to present our readers with the facts. . . . The word 'lie' conveys a moral as well as factual judgment. To accuse someone of lying is to impute a willful, deliberate attempt to deceive. It says he knowingly used a misrepresentation of the facts to mislead for his own purposes."

That Trump has consistently done just that seemed beside the point to Baker, whose position left many of his industry colleagues befuddled. Greg Sargent of *The Washington Post* observed, "The standard that Baker adopts—that there must be a provable intent to mislead—seems woefully inadequate to informing readers about what Trump is really up to." It also is a standard that no editor would apply to any ordinary person; but even if Trump himself does not respect the gravity of his office, some others are so awed by the position that they excuse the occupant's obvious failings.

In 2018, as Baker stepped down as editor to take a writing position, he issued a statement: "There has never been a more important time nor a greater demand for trusted, authoritative, objective journalism."

• • •

Even when Trump is no longer on the political scene, it seems likely his legacy will remain, that intentional falsehoods will continue to dominate political dialogue. And much of that has nothing to do with Trump. It has to do with the pouring of dark—or just purpose-motivated and shady—money into political advertising; with the growing recognition of the effectiveness of big (even publicly disproven) lies in driving a political agenda; with the commercial imperatives that give coverage of outlandish fabrications priority over substance and truth; with the online silos and publications that allow fanatics and fantasists to wall themselves off from reality; with the rise of a major so-called news network that traffics largely in propaganda; and with the domination of public space by companies, such as Facebook, that are fine with publishing outright lies. If there are any believers left in Brandeis's theory that good ideas and good information automatically will drive out bad, it is only because they have not yet awakened to the reality of the twenty-first century.

That reality raises numerous questions—concerning not just how we think about free speech but also how we think about mass media. For much of the last century the US was served well by a news media funded largely by advertisers and fueled by the public hunger for unbiased information. It is an open question of how well that commercially driven media—battered by unprecedented financial challenges—can meet the needs of the current age.

News media certainly will continue to play a huge role in our society. Indeed, much of the recent reporting done by the so-called mainstream press has been important, even essential, by any fair set of criteria. The question is whether that press, in a hostile political environment, can guide Americans through the fog of obfuscation that makes honest dialogue damnably difficult. The research suggests that the answer is no. Or at the very least that media outfits will need a lot of help.

In the last few years much of the most interesting journalism in the US has come from organizations such as ProPublica, The Center for Investigative Reporting, and The Marshall Project—nonprofit journalistic organizations that don't have to cater to commercial interests. The inevitable question is whether such models merit more intense consideration for foundations and other arms of civil society dedicated to fighting a culture of "alternative facts."

In *Post-Truth*, McIntyre observed, "In the past we have faced serious challenges—even to the notion of truth itself—

but never before have such challenges been so openly embraced as a strategy for the political subordination of reality. Thus what is striking about the idea of post-truth is not just that truth is being challenged, *but that it is being challenged as a mechanism for asserting political dominance.*"

It is nothing short of astonishing that the United States has become a place where former White House adviser Fiona Hill finds it necessary, during an impeachment inquiry, to lecture members of Congress on the consequences of spinning conspiracies out of Russian propaganda: "Some of you on this committee appear to believe that Russia and its security services did not conduct a campaign against our country—and that perhaps, somehow, for some reason, Ukraine did. This is a fictional narrative that has been perpetrated and propagated by the Russian security services themselves. . . . The impact of the successful 2016 Russian campaign remains evident today. Our nation is being torn apart. Truth is questioned. Our highly professional and expert career foreign service is being undermined."

Freedom House, a US-based human rights research and advocacy group, found 2019 to be the fourteenth consecutive year of decline in global freedom. It also rated freedom within the United States as significantly lower than in previous years, and lower than that of many of the United States' democratic peers.

"This problem," concluded Freedom House's 2019 report, "has been compounded by efforts to undermine democratic norms and standards within the United States over the past several years, including pressure on electoral integrity, judicial independence, and safeguards against corruption. Fierce rhetorical attacks on the press, the rule of law, and other pillars of democracy coming from American leaders, including the president himself, undermine the country's ability to persuade other governments to defend core human rights and freedoms, and are actively exploited by dictators and demagogues."

President Trump's attacks against the press have not been limited to conventional media. Angry that Twitter fact-checked his lie-filled diatribe about mail-in voting, he slammed Twitter for infringing upon his right to free speech. He threatened to retaliate by stripping Twitter of liability protection for false statements made on its site. Reporters pointed out that such an action was probably unconstitutional and could end up hurting Trump himself, who is notorious for making false accusations. Indeed, even as he threatened Twitter, Trump was falsely tweeting a suggestion that TV host Joe Scarborough was guilty of murder. The president seemingly had convinced himself that the First Amendment's purpose was to protect him from scrutiny for such horrific falsehoods. Nothing could be further from the truth—or from Brandeis's belief that free speech was emphatically not designed to protect lying presidents from the truth but to protect ordinary citizens from the "occasional tyrannies" of political leaders.

In his 1953 address at Harvard, newspaperman Palmer Hoyt essentially placed a bet on Brandeis—that, in the end, truth and justice would triumph. "It is my belief," said Hoyt, "that this nation is in transit . . . away from the outer darkness of fear, suspicion, and smear and toward the inner light of truth, fair play, and due process of law." He never could have foreseen all the forces that would take us in such a radically different direction.

He also did not reckon—nor has the United States as a nation reckoned—with the implications of a frightening but obvious truth, one that Trump and other great demagogues grasp intuitively: that lies swaddled in bigotry are almost impossible to dispel. A series of US governors rode that truth to regional glory—Ross Barnett, Lester Maddox, George Wallace, Orval Faubus, and the list goes on. Trump was more ambitious.

4

WHEN WORDS LEAD TO VIOLENCE

The years leading up to the Civil War saw the US at the height of partisanship. The divisions were less along party lines than along the line between profiteers from slavery and advocates for freedom. Senator Charles Sumner of Massachusetts fell victim to those intemperate times.

It was 1856, and Americans were fighting over the remaining territories acquired in the Louisiana Purchase. Two years earlier, Senator Stephen Douglas of Illinois and Senate Judiciary Committee chairman Andrew Butler of South Carolina had co-authored the Kansas-Nebraska Act of 1854. That legislation shattered the Missouri Compromise of 1820, opening the territories to slavery—if residents voted for it.

Many newly arrived Kansas residents turned out not to be residents at all. They were interlopers who had crossed the border from Missouri, then a slave state, to take up temporary residence in order to cast their vote for slavery in Kansas. The two sides fought a series of armed skirmishes that came to be called Bleeding Kansas.

Free state newspapers were early victims of the violence. As Gregg McCormick noted in the *Texas Law Review*, the legislature "made it a felony to 'print, or circulate, or publish, or aid in printing, circulating, or publishing' in the Territory 'any book, paper, pamphlet, magazine, handbill, or circular, containing any sentiment calculated to induce slaves to escape from the service of their masters.' Even more egregiously, the territorial legislature had made it criminal to assert that slavery did not legally exist in Kansas."

Against that violent, repressive, and highly polarized backdrop, Charles Sumner—a Harvard-educated lawyer who believed not only in abolition but in racial equality—took to the Senate to deliver a five-hour speech over two days. He titled his speech "The Crime Against Kansas."

Sumner minced no words. He unfavorably compared Douglas and Butler, architects of the Kansas-Nebraska Act, to the delusional Don Quixote and Sancho Panza. In Sumner's telling, Butler, who was not present for the speech, was besotted with slavery, which Sumner called Butler's "mistress."

> The senator from South Carolina . . . believes himself a chivalrous knight, with sentiments of honor and courage. Of course he has chosen a mistress to whom he has made his vows, and who, though ugly to others, is always lovely to him; though polluted in the sight of the world, is chaste

> in his sight—I mean the harlot Slavery. For her his tongue is always profuse with words. . . . If the slave States cannot enjoy . . . the full power in the National Territories to compel fellow-men to unpaid toil, to separate husband and wife, and to sell little children at the auction-block—then, sir, the chivalric senator will conduct the State of South Carolina out of the Union!

A few days later, Preston Smith Brooks, a pro-slavery congressman from South Carolina, sauntered into the Senate chamber. As the *New York Evening Post* reported the ensuing encounter: "Mr. Sumner was sitting in his place, writing very busily. Brooks approached him saying, 'Mr. Sumner, I have read your speech, twice. It is a libel on South Carolina, and on Mr. Butler, who is a relative of mine.' Mr. Sumner, who was still intently writing, knew nothing more. Brooks struck him with a heavy cane, upon which Sumner sprang from his seat to defend himself with such violence that the heavy desk before him was wrenched from the floor to which it was screwed. He was, however, so much staggered as to be rendered powerless, and the blows were repeated till he was senseless."

In his own account of the attack, as recounted by historian Manisha Sinha, Brooks wrote, "I struck him with my cane and gave him about 30 first rate stripes with a gutta percha cane . . . Every lick went where I intended. For about the first five of six licks he offered to make fight, but I plied him so rapidly that he did not touch me. Towards the last he bellowed like a calf."

The attack stunned the Senate and polarized the nation.

It led to Brooks's forced resignation and a fine, paid by his admirers. In his begrudging resignation speech that July, Brooks criticized Sumner for his "uncalled for libel on my State and my blood" and defended the life-threatening assault: "I should have forfeited my own self-respect, and perhaps the good opinion of my countrymen, if I had failed to resent such an injury by calling the offender in question to a personal account."

Brooks insisted he had meant "no disrespect to the Senate of the United States." He explained he had not challenged Sumner "to combat in the mode usually adopted" because he knew Sumner would not accept. And he underscored his restraint: "If I desired to kill the Senator, why did I not do it? You all admit that I had him in my power."

Commentators agreed the caning was unfortunate but sharply diverged on whom to blame. The southern press generally saw Brooks as a righteous man incited to unfortunate actions by intolerable provocations. The northern press saw Sumner's beating as a flagrant violation of his constitutionally granted freedom of speech. A minority took a middle course, condemning the violence but also criticizing abolitionists.

The *New York Herald* thundered that Brooks's violence "has made a hero, a lion and a martyr of Senator Sumner, and has given to the anti-slavery coalition, languishing for lack of capital, the very thing which they desired—a living 'raw head and bloody bones' with which to . . . arouse [a] fanatical spirit of cooperation against what they designate the 'despotic slave oligarchy' of the South."

The *Richmond Enquirer* hailed Brooks as a hero: "We consider the act good in conception, better in execution, and best of all in consequence. These vulgar Abolitionists in the Senate are getting above themselves. They have been humored until they forget their position. . . . They must be lashed into submission."

Brooks's home state newspaper, the *Columbian Carolinian*, reveled in the encounter: "Immediately upon reception of the news on Saturday last, a most enthusiastic meeting was convened in the town of Newberry. . . . Complimentary [*sic*] resolutions were introduced by General A. C. Garlington. . . . The meeting voted [Brooks] a handsome gold-headed cane. . . . We heard one of Carolina's truest and most honored matrons from Mr. Brooks' district send a message to him by Maj. Simpson, saying 'that the ladies of the South would send him hickory sticks, with which to chastise Abolitionists and Red Republicans whenever he wanted them.'"

It went on to say: "Here in Columbia, a handsome sum, headed by the Governor of the State, has been subscribed, for the purpose of presenting Mr. Brooks with a splendid silver pitcher, goblet and stick. . . . And, to add the crowning glory to the good work, the slaves of Columbia have already a handsome subscription, and will present an appropriate token of their regard, to him who has made the first practical issue for their preservation and protection in their rights and enjoyments as the happiest laborers on the face of the globe."

Brooks was reelected within weeks of his resignation. He died the following year from croup at the age of thirty-seven. Sumner, after a months-long, difficult recovery, returned to the Senate, where he served with distinction. He died of a heart attack in March 1874 at the age of sixty-three.

• • •

None of this is to say we are on the verge of a second civil war. Relations in the US are not quite that bleak. Nor is there a national dispute over an explosive issue that could pit state against state in a fight to the death. But our union is certainly divided, in much the same way and along similar lines to those of the 1850s. We are in profound disagreement about what the United States represents and what its future face should be. We have racial arsonists, the likes of Unite the Right convener Jason Kessler, who see these next few decades as perhaps the last opportunity to secure this country's survival as a nation dedicated to white supremacy. And we have a chief executive who is a singularly polarizing personality, proudly exploiting those differences that already divide us.

One could arguably describe Abraham Lincoln as a similar figure. His crusade against slavery's expansion was profoundly divisive in a country where many citizens saw owning other human beings as their God-given right and the key to their personal prosperity.

Although the US no longer has legal slavery, it does have easily demonized minorities—who provide great fodder for lies swaddled in bigotry. The mortal threat, as defined by Trump and many of his acolytes, consists of invading hordes intent on infesting us from the south, religious fanatics eying us from the Middle East, homegrown socialists destroying us from within, and green-energy types standing in the way of making America "great again." For the large number of Americans who accept his essential message as true, specific—even easily disprovable—facts become rather beside the point.

In other words, among a culturally and politically polarized electorate, what most determines how you view reality is which side you are on—not which side accurately reports, and responsibly responds to, facts. And in a society in which one's view of reality is hugely influenced by one's political affiliation (which side you have chosen), even the most outlandish notions easily find acceptance—if they are pushed by someone perceived as a faithful comrade in arms.

Andries du Toit, director of the Institute for Poverty, Land, and Agrarian Studies at South Africa's University of the Western Cape, asked in his article on openDemocracy in 2017: "How do we make sense of the fact that we are in a world where there are significant numbers of people who really believe—*and who want to believe!*—that [Hillary] Clinton was running a Satanic paedophile ring out of a pizza restaurant in Washington?"

The supposed villains in such conspiracy theories, noted Du Toit, vary according to the country. In Europe, they might be members of the so-called Illuminati. In South Africa, they might swirl around billionaires Anton Rupert or George Soros.

Always, the tales involved colorful and compelling stories that "not only purport to explain the world . . . but that also systematically 'poison the well' against competing versions of the truth." The bizarre narratives attracted believers, argued Du Toit, because "they make some kind of emotional and political sense." They took popular grievances and gave them a focus and rationale, even as they fostered a sense of belonging, along with a polarizing us-against-them worldview.

Du Toit's point—that people are more interested in belonging than in truth, more inclined to wallow in collective grievance than to accept a disempowering reality, more invested in raging against an oppressive, unfair system than in scrutinizing inconvenient facts—goes a long way toward explaining why objective reality matters so little in much public discourse.

Daily Mail columnist Melanie Phillips hypothesized that many widely debunked conspiracy theories (including those spun around the deaths of President John Kennedy and Princess Diana) "play on the widespread belief—which has taken hold since Vietnam and Watergate—that the ruling class represents a malign conspiracy against the public."

Science writer Keith Kloor has argued much the same point, noting, "Trump's winning strategy centered on demonizing his opponent and delegitimizing his critics, such as those pesky, fact-checking journalists. This required an overarching narrative—of a corrupt, entrenched political establishment, which Hillary Clinton embodies."

The delegitimization of objective truth is also abetted by the belief that "science" is just another word for "opinion." When the president of the United States (who prior to becoming president called climate change "a total, and very expensive, hoax") insists that climate "changes both ways," he replaces a healthy culture of scientific skepticism with an unhealthy ethos of uninformed skepticism about and rejection of science itself. That rejection leads to policies that undermine science, just as other, more blatantly political policies sideline objective truth.

The politicization of scientific agencies, incidentally, did not begin with the Trump administration. The Union of Concerned Scientists reviewed the work of the EPA in 2007, during the Bush administration, and found political influence to be rampant. As the UCS put it, "hundreds of scientists reported political interference in their work, significant barriers to the free communication of scientific results, and concerns about the agency's effectiveness."

Trump just took things to another level—which is one reason why reversing his initial messaging on COVID-19 was so difficult.

As of early 2020, a Columbia University–based center looking at the "silencing" of science has counted more than four hundred separate instances since Trump's election that meet its criteria—meaning "any action that has the effect of restricting or prohibiting scientific research, education, or discussion, or the publication or use of scientific information."

A 2019 report from the National Task Force on Rule of Law and Democracy, at New York University School of Law's Brennan Center for Justice, concluded that over "the last few decades, the safeguards meant to keep government research objective and publicly accessible have been steadily weakening. . . . This trend has culminated in the efforts of the current administration not only to politicize scientific and technical research on a range of topics, but also, at times, to undermine the value of objective facts themselves."

• • •

In November 2019, the Southern Poverty Law Center released a report that was notable for the fact that virtually no one was shocked by what it revealed. The report, presented on the SPLC blog *Hatewatch* and titled "Stephen Miller's Affinity for White Nationalism Revealed in Leaked Emails," detailed Miller's emails to editors at an "alt-right" website. It called Miller's focus "strikingly narrow" and noted that more than 80 percent of his emails to Breitbart News Network's editors "relate to or appear on threads relating to the subjects of race or immigration." The SPLC summed up its research with: "In the run-up to the 2016 election, White House senior policy adviser Stephen Miller promoted white nationalist literature, pushed racist immigration stories and obsessed over the loss of Confederate symbols after Dylann Roof's murderous rampage, according to leaked emails."

The SPLC also drew a direct connection between Miller's apparent fascination with white supremacist ideology and "the extremist, anti-immigrant ideology that undergirds the policies he has helped create as an architect of Donald Trump's presidency."

White House spokesperson Hogan Gidley responded by suggesting the criticism of Miller was nothing more than anti-Semitism: "What deeply concerns me is how so many on the left are allowed to spread vile anti-Semitism and consistently attack proud Jewish members of this administration." It was a textbook example of the "I'm going to ignore your deeply damning claims and just call you a bigot" defense.

• • •

In an era when the president of the United States prefers fantasies to fact, when political discourse has degenerated to the point that name-calling tweets pass for argument, and when one of the president's closest advisers is a barely closeted white nationalist, it was probably to be expected that hate speech and hate crimes would resurge.

In a November 2017 article published in *The Conversation*, PhD candidate Nadia Naffi reported on a six-fold increase in what she called "the amount of intolerant and hate speech in social media postings by Canadians between November 2015 and November 2016." Naffi acknowledged that some analysts blamed Trump for the increase but suggested there was plenty of blame to go around—including negative media coverage of Syrian refugees in Canada and renewed efforts by extremist political parties and right-wing activists.

A report released in April 2018 by the Council on American-Islamic Relations detailed an increase in both anti-Muslim bias incidents (up 17 percent) and hate crimes (up 15 percent nationwide in 2017) that coincided with the rise of Donald Trump. "Trump's xenophobic rhetoric, both prior to and during the course of his presidency, emboldened those who sought to express their anti-Muslim bias and provided a veneer of legitimacy to bigotry in the public sphere," concluded the report. In an update that July, CAIR revealed that "anti-Muslim bias incidents and hate crimes are up 83 and 21 percent respectively," compared to the first quarter of 2018.

Other studies showed the same upward trend. A 2019 research paper chronicled a doubling of anti-Muslim hate crimes since the beginning of the Trump campaign. The "increase in anti-Muslim sentiment in the US since the start of Trump's presidential campaign [compared to during the Obama and Bush presidencies] has been concentrated in counties with high Twitter usage," observed Karsten Müller, a research associate at Princeton University, and Carlo Schwarz, of the University of Warwick. The rise in hate crimes, they added, was "particularly striking because Bush's term included a temporary ten-fold increase in such crimes following the 9/11 terror attacks, the largest spike since the beginning of the FBI records in 1990."

Analysis of FBI statistics by the Simon Wiesenthal Center, a Jewish human rights organization, also showed a steady increase in hate crimes. In a statement to the House Judiciary Committee in April 2019, the center concluded, "The statistics confirm that victims were most often targeted by race/ethnicity with religiously based crimes being the second most reported category. The highest proportion of racially targeted victims, almost 50%, were victims of 'anti-black or African American bias' while the highest proportion of religious targets, almost 60%, were victims of 'anti-Jewish bias.'"

Brian Levin, director of the Center for the Study of Hate

and Extremism at California State University, San Bernardino, believes society is especially vulnerable to crimes of hate and resentment. "A fragmented, polarized society is finding a home, an echo chamber online," Levin said in an interview with the *Daily Breeze* of Torrance, California. "The biggest risk we face is from the fragments, the loners that cuts [*sic*] across all ideologies."

The rise in public bigotry, researchers concede, is not just due to what many now call the Trump Effect. Public incivility, the dread of a demographically changing US, and the sprouting of safe spaces for bigotry online are all implicated in the escalation of hateful speech and behavior. But even though it is impossible to say, with precision, just what influence Trump has had, there are plenty of examples of public haters tipping their hats to the president, as professors Griffin Edwards and Stephen Rushin have pointed out. Their 2018 study listed a number of perpetrators who paid tribute to Trump, including men who brutally assailed a sleeping Mexican immigrant in Boston, assailants who stapled a slur on the stomach of undocumented immigrant in Michigan, and the mass murderer in Christchurch, New Zealand. "While it does not rival the spike in hate crimes after September 11th," argued Edwards and Rushin, "there is evidence to suggest the Trump Effect may have contributed to a statistically significant uptick in the number of hate crimes rivaled by few other events in modern American history."

In the end, the problem with hate speech—and hate crimes—extends far beyond Donald Trump. There is little doubt that he has emboldened a certain set of people—not just in the US but across the globe. Yet the polarization and fear he epitomizes would have existed even had Trump not entered politics, and will exist long after he is gone.

The technology and the anonymity that have supercharged the hate speech movement have nothing really to do with Trump. He just happens to be the first US president to have figured out how formidable a weapon Twitter can be in the hands of a bigot who has the attention of the world.

The US, as envisioned by the Founders, did not have internationally available hate-filled silos into which psychologically troubled would-be mass murderers and angry, wounded chauvinists could safely crawl while suckling and stoking their resentments before unleashing their hate on the world.

This unprecedented and unforeseen reality raises difficult questions about how we handle potentially harmful speech that has no apparent social value—speech that, for all of Brandeis's naïve idealism, can easily coexist with and even triumph over the more rational speech that supposedly would render it moot.

We revere our First Amendment and its almost absolute promise of freedom of speech. As political scientists Dennis Chong and Morris Levy have pointed out, Americans "are more supportive of free speech than are the respondents of any other country. Citizens in other nations are significantly more inclined to identify exclusions to free speech, to favor restrictions on speech targeting racial and ethnic minorities, and to balance the value of equality against the right to free expression."

But American feelings are not static. As Chong and Levy also note, many Americans are growing weary of hate speech—and questioning just how much protection it should receive: "There have been massive gains in tolerance for atheists, communists, homosexuals, and even militarists since the mid-1970s." But tolerance for racist speech has shown no such trend. Indeed, it "has declined slightly over the past decade." The decline has been even sharper among college graduates, who are "about 15 points less tolerant of racist speech than they were in 1980." Americans also are not particularly accepting of the notion that Muslim clerics should be allowed to "preach hatred of America."

Increasingly, thinkers across the political spectrum are seeking ways to preserve free speech while also minimizing the damage of particularly poisonous speech to our democracy. They are questioning whether a key assumption—that protecting such vibrant expression is central to democratic governance—really makes sense, especially when much of this speech does not communicate ideas but simply spreads hatred and animosity, and has about as much to do with constructive debate as did the caning of Charles Sumner in 1856.

5

WHAT THE FOUNDERS NEVER IMAGINED

Once upon a time there was a United States in which mass media did not exist, in which average citizens had no idea who might be capable of national leadership, in which women could not vote, nonwhites could not fully participate, and direct democracy was viewed with horror. For that country, a group of people, who came to be known as Founders, established a system for electing a president. And the nation has been heroically, and often vainly, trying to make that system work ever since.

Because the Founders did not trust citizens to elect a leader, the task of winnowing down the candidates was given over to electors. These electors presumably would be better informed than the hoi polloi and would make more judicious, wiser decisions—leaving Congress to pick a president from among the best the US had to offer.

As fate would have it, virtually every assumption made by the Founders turned out to be false. As researcher Rachel Tropp put it in the *Harvard Political Review*, "[The] Electoral College has been greatly distorted by the rose-colored lenses of history."

So how did we get here?

Delegates to the Constitutional Convention had reached a stalemate. They had considered and rejected having state legislators or governors choose a president. They had also thought about having fifteen congressmen, chosen by lot, do the honor; but that option failed because they realized that if the lot selected "unworthy men, an unworthy Executive must be saddled on the Country," observed Elbridge Gerry from Massachusetts during the Federal Convention. Joseph Connor of the magazine *American History* reported, "On August 31, 1787, after more than three months of deliberations, delegates referred the question of how to pick a president to the Convention's Committee of Eleven on Postponed Matters." The committee decided to go with a system of electors, whose means of selection would be left to state legislators.

Other methods had been considered and discarded. One problem with popular election was that delegates "could not imagine how, in a decentralized nation like the United States, the people could ever make an effective choice," noted historian and political scientist Jack Rakove. "Once the country looked for a successor to Washington, there simply would not be enough genuine 'national characters' . . . to enable the electorate to produce a majority decision."

As Joseph Connor added in his report, Elbridge Gerry

worried that "pretended patriots" would dupe the masses if ever the public was entrusted with such a momentous decision. And "George Mason of Virginia derided as 'unnatural' handing that choice to voters, which he likened to asking a blind man to choose a color."

The idea of election by Congress also had its drawbacks. "First, and most important," observed Rakove, "it could not satisfy the one concern that operated as an independent variable driving all other calculations: the framers' underlying desire to make the president as independent of legislative control and manipulation as possible." The Electoral College scheme "was also subject to telling objections, but its defects and disadvantages seemed less worrisome than those which weighed against the other modes." It was, in short, seen as the best of several bad prospective models.

"The Framers envisioned that the electors who would make this momentous decision every four years would be nonpartisan free agents acting with an eye toward nothing except the public weal. The electors were to be the nation's best and brightest, individuals," observed Connor. In the words of Alexander Hamilton, individuals "most likely to possess the information and discernment requisite to such complicated investigations."

They would also not necessarily be charged with the final choice. Their job was more akin to that of a screening committee. In a process in which political parties played no role, the Electoral College would choose, say, five finalists, and from among those the House would name a president and a vice president.

As historian Andrew Shankman summed up the system,

"each state appointed electors equal to its number of senators (2) plus representatives, apportioned at a ratio of 1 for every 30,000 residents. Each elector cast two votes for president and at least one of those votes had to be for someone outside the elector's state. If someone received the most votes and a majority, he became president. The second highest became vice president."

By 1796, two political parties had come to dominate. Shankman noted, "With large regional, even national, voting blocks, it was suddenly highly likely that the leader of one of the two parties would gain a majority in the Electoral College. The Electoral College would now do what the Founders never imagined it should routinely do—determine the presidency. And the new president's most powerful critic, the leader of the opposition party, would likely get the second most electoral votes, become the vice president, and bring bitter partisan rancor into the heart of the executive branch."

Almost immediately the system imploded. In 1796, John Adams became president and his opponent, Thomas Jefferson, the second-highest vote getter, became vice president. Matters grew even worse in 1800, when Thomas Jefferson and Aaron Burr received the same number of electoral votes. The matter was thrown to the House, which was deeply divided. Finally, on the thirty-sixth ballot, after much rancorous political maneuvering, Jefferson was awarded the office.

The fix was the Twelfth Amendment, ratified in 1804, which separated the ballots for president and vice president. But that did not address the underlying problem, which was that the system was fundamentally flawed as an effort at democratic governance.

"In abandoning the Founders' vision for the Electoral College," according to Shankman, "Americans were admitting that they did not live in the sort of republic where the Founders' Electoral College made sense: one where virtuous gentlemen pursued the singular unifying public good about which they all agreed. In altering the Electoral College as they did, Americans of the early nineteenth century left us a hybrid and confused version of the original. Requiring electors to vote for a president and a vice president on a single ticket was a concession that party political conflict was never going away."

Among the many arguments made against the Electoral College is that its very structure was an accommodation to slavery. It is clearly true that the formula for allocating members in the House of Representatives originally counted three-fifths of nonvoting slaves as part of the voting population—even though it was slave owners, not enslaved people, who exercised that three-fifths of a vote. That gave slave states unmerited representation. Since the Electoral College system was built on that immoral compromise (deciding the number of electors by adding each state's allocation of House members to its two senators), the Electoral College similarly magnified the power of voters in slave-owning states. (The Permanent Apportionment Act of 1929 capped the number of representatives in the House at 435, which also capped the number of electors, since their number is derived principally from the allocation of senators and representatives.)

As constitutional scholar Akhil Reed Amar argued in an

op-ed in the *New York Times*, the most significant political divide at the time of the 1787 Constitutional Convention was "between North and South and was all about slavery." Because the South's population was relatively small (if slaves, who could not vote, were excluded), southern presidential candidates would always lose a direct election, conjectured James Madison. But if somehow slaves could be indirectly counted, Southerners might go along. The Electoral College provided a way to do that, as it created a system with a huge proslavery tilt. Consequently, "every president until Abraham Lincoln was either a Southerner or a Northerner who was willing (while president) to accommodate the slaveholding South," argued Amar.

Historian Sean Wilentz, in another *New York Times* op-ed, took aim at that argument. In his view, creation of the Electoral College had virtually nothing to do with garnering southern support. In the initial vote, he pointed out, Southerners repudiated the system: "the only states voting 'nay' were North Carolina, South Carolina, and Georgia—the three most ardently proslavery states in the convention." The reason, wrote Wilentz, is that Southerners feared that electors would be subject to corruption: "There are ample grounds for criticizing the Constitution's provisions for electing the president. . . . But the myth that the Electoral College began as a slaveholders' instrument needs debunking."

From my perspective, the question of how much the Electoral College was rooted in a compromise over slavery, while intellectually interesting, is somewhat beside the point. Yes, the very structure of the Electoral College had appeasement of slave owners at its heart. But that changed following the

Civil War when the Fifteenth Amendment eliminated "race, color, or previous condition of servitude" as a justification for denying supposedly free blacks the right to vote.

The problem is that the South did not honor that amendment. So blacks continued to be counted in the apportionment for congressmen (this time in their full number, as opposed to three-fifths)—and therefore for president electors. But blacks, for the most part, were denied access to the ballot—generally brutally. Thus former slave-holding states were granted an even larger representational advantage, as white voters in that region got the benefit of a large black population but continued to vote in direct opposition to that population's welfare. In short, once the three-fifths system was abandoned, segregationists—by defying the law—exerted even greater unmerited influence. And they did so for fully a century after the Civil War.

Patrick Rael, in *Picking the President*, commented on that irony: at the turn of the last century, the white South received a 7 percent bump in the Electoral College because of its "largely disenfranchised African Americans. . . . One might have thought that ending slavery would have ended the compromise embodied in the three-fifths clause—a system that John Quincy Adams came to call 'morally and politically vicious.' It was not to be. Of the many paradoxes to the 'freedom' that followed slavery, one of the most neglected may be this: in the era of Jim Crow, ending slavery only made the white South stronger."

Even after the Voting Rights Act was passed in 1965, countless southern districts continued to deny, or drastically restrict, the right of blacks to vote. To a remarkable extent, such efforts continue to this day, which is why gerrymandering and voter suppression remain such potent and divisive issues.

Indeed, one of the reasons so many blacks fled the South (and are now arguably overrepresented in large urban centers in such states as Illinois, New York, and California) is because those southern, rural areas treated blacks horribly. The irony is that many of the states they fled because of blatant discrimination are the very states that the Electoral College (augmented by winner-take-all allocation schemes) rewards with extra votes.

Benjamin James Waddell argued that point in an article for openDemocracy, detailing the massive exodus of not just blacks during the so-called Great Migration but also other minority groups. As Waddell points out, minorities of every stripe had good reasons for leaving their homes in rural and small-town America. Jobs were vanishing on reservations, motivating Native Americans to leave. Many Asian Americans who had been forced to abandon their homes by the internment policies of World War II opted not to return but instead to make a life elsewhere. Huge numbers of Mexican Americans and other Latinos also decided they would be better off in large urban areas. That mass exodus, argues Waddell, "should have penalized rural states by reducing their share of electoral votes, but it did just the opposite. As a result of migration out of rural areas, the Electoral College currently overvalues rural states at a rate of roughly 3 to 1."

Blacks, Latinos, Asian Americans, and Native Americans all tend to vote Democratic. But instead of voting in rural areas, they are now voting disproportionately in big cities and big states, meaning that their votes matter a lot less. By moving from Wyoming to California, for example, a voter loses roughly 66 percent of the value of his or her vote, argues Waddell.

In short, the problem with the Electoral College is not that it was forged through concessions to slavery; little in US history has escaped slavery's taint. The problem is that it continues to revictimize voters who have already been victimized by discrimination.

But even putting the issues of racial and ethnic discrimination aside entirely, is there really a compelling justification for valuing certain votes—purely because of where they come from—over others? Are we really a better nation because a handful of voters in, for example, Florida or North Carolina have more say than hundreds of thousands in California?

The problem, as I alluded to earlier, is not wholly due to the Electoral College. Most states, following the dictates of political parties, award all electoral votes on a winner-take-all basis—a practice some critics believe to be unconstitutional—thereby magnifying the unfairness of the Electoral College.

Given that the Electoral College so blatantly rejects the "one person, one vote" principle, and given that it also has worked precisely the opposite to the way the Founders believed that it would—winnowing candidates down to the best of the best—why do we keep it around?

The short answer is that it would just be too much trouble to change it. The slightly longer answer is that it works just fine if you like its results. If your dream is to have a president, elected by a hostile minority, unashamedly impose his will on the majority, then the Electoral College makes perfect sense.

• • •

In reflecting on the Donald Trump presidency, historian Manisha Sinha observed that Trump had something in common with Andrew Johnson, who also became the subject of an impeachment effort. "Both presidencies began with a whiff of illegitimacy hanging over them: Johnson's because he became president when Lincoln was assassinated, Mr. Trump's because he won the Electoral College despite having nearly three million fewer popular votes than his opponent, the largest losing margin of any president who actually won the election. The size of the gap did not bode well for American democracy."

In 1996, long before the idea of a Trump presidency seemed possible, Matthew M. Hoffman wrote a *Yale Law Journal* article—"The Illegitimate President: Minority Vote Dilution and the Electoral College"—warning that the Electoral College played into the hands of polarizing politicians. Hoffman observed that racially polarized appeals to constituents had been a defining feature of presidential campaigns for half a century, ever since the rise of the so-called Dixiecrats. Those appeals—overt and covert—to racism, argued Hoffman, virtually guaranteed voters would be divided along racial lines. In the winner-take-all voting schemes in place in most states, polarized voting totally shut black voters out of the process of electing America's presidents. "This problem is most acute in the states of the former Confederacy. . . . In these states, African-American voters have little or no hope of choosing even a single member of the electoral college," pointed out Hoffman.

In other words, the issue of an illegitimate presidency was essentially foretold. We chose, as a country, to close our eyes to its inevitability. Nonetheless, many thoughtful people sincerely believe the Electoral College is the best that we can do.

In *Picking the President*, historian Andrew Meyer argued that without the Electoral College, "candidates would focus almost entirely on the densely populated coasts to the exclusion of the interior, and on urban centers to the exclusion of more sparsely settled rural districts. By giving disproportionate leverage to more rural and sparsely populated states, the Electoral College forces candidates to wage truly national campaigns and to float policies that can win the votes of more marginalized citizens."

In an op-ed published in 2000 in *The Wall Street Journal*, historian Joseph Ellis put forth a variation of the "It's just too hard to change" argument. To jettison the Electoral College, he asserted, would also require changing other things, including allowing for the plurality vote winner to become president, or allowing for a runoff, or revising constitutional provisions on how the House votes: "The prospect of the current Congress managing its way through this political minefield is difficult to imagine."

John Yoo and James Phillips, in an April 2019 editorial in the *Los Angeles Times*, dismissed calls for the elimination of the Electoral College as simply part of a partisan Democratic agenda: "Democrats defend their partisan agenda by arguing that the electoral college violates democracy. It is true that the system at least dilutes democracy. Critics, however, ignore that much of that effect is because of the states themselves. They choose to award their electoral votes using a winner-take-all approach. Regardless of whether Trump won Pennsylvania by 10,000 votes or by 500,000 votes, he received its 20 electoral votes and Hillary Clinton got zero."

In a 2003 article in *Perspectives on Political Science* ("The Electoral College and the Development of American Democracy"), Professor Gary Glenn made the convoluted—and, I believe, ridiculous—argument that "facts" are not what most people think they are. People ae wrong, he argued, in assuming that "'more' popular votes means 'more' votes counted as a national total." Instead, in a presidential election, he wrote, "more" means something totally different from what it means in any other context: "In this election, and only in the presidential election, the Constitutional system does not throw all the popular votes into one national pot and then count them. Rather we count them by fifty-one separate election districts. And the candidate who gets more popular votes when the popular votes are counted by states (federally) wins. Always. No exceptions."

Glenn compared it to the World Series, where the winner "must win four games out of seven, not score the most total runs in the seven games."

Of course most Americans quite reasonably don't view a presidential election as a best-four-out-of-seven series of dice tosses. And as for whether some of the complaints are partisan in nature, obviously they are—since the present system currently favors Republicans. But just because Democrats don't see the current system as operating in their favor doesn't mean they don't have a valid point.

Also, it simply makes no sense to say that candidates, competing in a truly national election, would ignore the millions of voters who don't live in highly urban areas. They would still need those rural and small-state votes to win.

Even such a reform-minded critic as Amar acknowledged that any "reforms might backfire, with unforeseen and adverse consequences. The Electoral College is the devil we know."

The argument for keeping a broken system (and one that, indeed, has been broken from the beginning) because it's just too damn hard to change is certainly not an argument that bodes well for a nation that supposedly believes in the efficacy and ethics of democracy—unless we either don't believe in democracy or only believe in a kind of situational democracy.

As Andrew Shankman pointed out, "Trump supporters demanded that electors obey the popular vote within their states. At the state level the popular vote must be respected so that at the national level the popular vote can be ignored. This selective devotion to the popular vote is a legacy of the confusion that resulted when the Founders created an institution that made sense only for conditions that it quickly turned out did not exist."

As for the argument that the Electoral College ensures that the needs of smaller states are met, that is just so much nonsense. As Rachel Tropp said, "Some . . . argue that the Electoral College allows small states like New Hampshire to gain critical importance in the electoral process, but this ignores the fact that under the current system, the other 12 smallest states are entirely ignored. In 2012, these states received no significant campaign events due to their safely partisan leanings. In fact, only 12 states received any significant events, lessening Electoral College proponents' claim of fairness. There is no good reason why winning by a slim margin within a few states' boundaries should override the will of a majority of the people in the country, especially when the margins of victory in many states are so slim they hardly represent a mandate or clear preference at all." (Much the same argument could be made about the primary/caucus calendar favoring New Hampshire and Iowa, but that is an argument for another time.)

Tropp went on to point out that Trump's victory in some swing states was razor thin. Trump "won Michigan by 10,704 votes, less than a quarter of a percentage point, contributing 16 electoral votes to his success. . . . If a mere 5,353 voters went the other way, Clinton would have won the state, whereas in consistently blue or red states, much larger margins are completely discounted once a majority is reached."

So to repeat: Does any rational person truly believe that the ends of democracy are best served by giving individual voters in such states as Florida, New Hampshire, Nevada, and Wisconsin so much more power than their counterparts in California or New York?

One could, I suppose, argue that the Electoral College provides a superior form of democracy, but not without making a corollary argument that there is something superior about the judgment of voters in such states, which, of course, raises the uncomfortable question of what makes their judgment superior.

The Founders did not shy away from the issue of superior judgment. They agreed that certain voters were superior to others, and that, to the extent possible, decisions about democracy should be left in those superior voters' hands. Those preferred, superior voters were male, white, Christian freeholders—landowners.

Thank God we have gotten away from that kind of thinking. Or have we?

6

SHAKING UP THE SENATE

Over the years, numerous people have criticized the Electoral College as an affront to democracy, and some have tried to change it. In September 1969, the House passed the Bayh-Celler Amendment 339–70. The measure, which called for direct popular election of the president, was approved "in such overwhelming fashion that even the measure's supporters are surprised—and pleased," reported the Associated Press. The lopsided House vote, added the AP, raised hopes that the proposal could pass the Senate, be ratified by the states, and soon become the Twenty-Sixth Amendment to the Constitution.

The optimism did not last. A year later, on October 5, the Senate dropped the effort. As the *Baltimore Sun* put it, "With . . . a third attempt to end debate certain to fail tomorrow, advocates of popular election of the President agreed to let the constitutional amendment be shelved after two conferences aimed at reaching a compromise failed."

"We're just not going to be able to shut off this filibuster," said Senator Birch Bayh, the bill's chief sponsor. He called the outcome "rather depressing." *New York Times* columnist Tom Wicker wrote, "Here, in sum, is a blatant case of a little band of willful men who fear, and are therefore thwarting, both popular will and the political process that they extol."

No legislative effort since then has fared any better. In February 2018, a group of law firms led by the League of United Latin American Citizens and prominent attorney David Boies announced four lawsuits against the winner-take-all systems governing the allocation of Electoral College votes in forty-eight states. Bois called the winner-take-all system "a clear violation of the principle of one person, one vote," adding: "We filed these cases in order to uphold the rights of every citizen. All Americans deserve to have their votes count."

Former Massachusetts governor William Weld, a challenger to Donald Trump for the 2020 Republican presidential nomination, was a party to the suit. He argued in a *USA Today* op-ed, co-authored with legal scholar and co-plaintiff Sanford Levinson, that "the consequences of striking down winner-take-all would benefit all voters, whatever their political party, by making every state a battleground state. They would be lavished with attention, and they would turn out to vote because they would feel like their votes matter."

For all the criticism rightly leveled at the Electoral College and its associated winner-take-all scheme, the Senate has largely escaped serious reform efforts. And the Senate—in case you haven't noticed—is much less representative than the Electoral College.

The United States is a famously and proudly diverse country. But because of the two-senators-per-state rule, the United States has become a country overrepresented by—and forced to cater to—the least diverse and least representative portions of the country.

Consider this: the least populous twenty-six states have roughly one-sixth the population of the most populous twenty-four. As a result, absolute authority for federal judicial appointments, and executive office confirmations, is in the hands of senators representing only 17.57 percent of the population.

In other words, 82.43 percent of Americans (according to the July 2018 population estimates) have no voice over some of the most important decisions affecting their lives. Put another way, a vote by Americans who belong to that privileged 18 percent is worth roughly 5.7 times the value of a vote by the other 82 percent. Consequently, senators who represent just over 57 million Americans can legally and freely impose their will on those who represent 269 million. And largely as a result of slavery and its fraught aftermath (which included institutionalized Jim Crow and flagrant discrimination against people of color), the composition of that electorally advantaged 18 percent is quite different from the composition of the rest of the US.

Blacks make up just short of 11 percent of the total residents of the twenty-six least populous states. They constitute over 15 percent of the population of the most populous states. Ethnic minorities (classified by the Census as Latinos, blacks, Asian Americans, and Native Americans) are not particularly well integrated into the populations of the country's least populous states—in those states (Wyoming, Vermont, Alaska, North Dakota, and South Dakota), there are 39 whites for every black person. In the five most populous states (California, Texas, Florida, New York, and Pennsylvania), you find 4.5 whites for every black person. The five least populous states have fifteen times the number of non-Hispanics as they have Hispanics. In the most populous states, the ratio is 1.5 to 1. We are talking about two very different Americas, with the most segregated America empowered to impose its will on the most diverse. It is a power that is used routinely, and its exercise tears at the very fabric of an increasingly diverse nation.

As journalist Parker Richards noted in *The Atlantic* in 2018, "Brett Kavanaugh was confirmed to the United States Supreme Court by a vote of 50–48, with one senator absent and one abstaining. Only one Democrat, Joe Manchin of West Virginia, voted with the solidly Republican majority, which represented just 44 percent of the country's population. Indeed, when Americans last voted for their senators . . . Democrats won the popular vote by more than 8 percent. It's that disproportionality—and the reality that a majority of the country's population is represented by just 18 senators—that is driving concerns about the Senate's ability to function as a representative body in a changing America."

A study released in 2009 by the NAACP Legal Defense and Educational Fund ("Post-Racial America? Not Yet") reported that racially polarized voting remains an unfortunate reality. Candidates favored by whites were almost invariably shunned by blacks, said the report. And when candidates were of different races, voters tended to go with their own kind. In Alabama in 2008, Barack Obama received only 10 percent of the white vote, whereas in 2004 John Kerry, a white Democrat, had received 19 percent. Much the same was true in Louisiana, where Kerry received 24 percent of the white vote and Obama only 14 percent.

The report went on to say, "Nationally, 95 percent of blacks voted for President Obama, but only 43 percent of whites voted for him. Whites were the only racial group that did not cast a majority of their votes for President Obama."

Despite the dream many have of a colorblind America, we don't have one now. "While most Americans believe that they are able to treat everyone equally," Arusha Gordon and Ezra Rosenberg stated in 2015 in the *Michigan Journal of Race & Law*, "more than seventy percent of Americans possess some level of implicit bias based on race."

In a country with highly racially polarized voting patterns, our insistence on putting power in the hands of an unrepresentative minority is an invitation to social discontent—and perhaps a looming disaster.

In a 2004 article in *Harper's Magazine*, scholar and author Richard N. Rosenfeld called for the abolition of the Senate: "In America today, U.S. senators from the twenty-six smallest states, representing a mere 18 percent of the nation's population, hold a majority in the United States Senate, and, therefore, under the Constitution, regardless of what the President, the House of Representatives, or even an overwhelming majority of the American people wants, nothing becomes law if those senators object. The result has been what one would expect: The less populous states have extracted benefits from the rest of the nation quite out of proportion to their populations."

In 2019, in the *American University Law Review*, professor Eric W. Orts observed, "At the founding, the ratio of voting weight in the Senate between citizens in the smallest state of Delaware and the largest state of Virginia was around nine to one or twelve to one, depending on whether slaves are counted. James Madison predicted that this inequality would get worse, and he was right. As new states were added, and as people multiplied and migrated, the ratios of voting inequality of citizens in the smallest and largest states widened. Today, the ratio of voting weight of citizens in the smallest state of Wyoming compared with those in the largest state of California has grown to *sixty-seven to one*." Orts noted that it is "now possible for senators representing only one-fifth of the population to pass a bill or confirm a Supreme Court justice."

Justices Brett Kavanaugh and Neil Gorsuch, he added, "share the dubious distinction . . . of being both confirmed by senators representing a minority of the population and nominated by a president who himself won election with only a minority of the total vote. They are the first of what we might call minority-minority justices." And this is in a nation that, without any sense of irony, calls itself a democracy.

How did we end up with such an insane and inequitable system?

It all began in 1787, at the Constitutional Convention in Philadelphia. Prior to acceptance of what eventually became known as the Great Compromise (whose leading exponent was Roger Sherman, a delegate from Connecticut), the convention had pondered and deadlocked over two competing plans. The Virginia Plan, pushed by James Madison (of Virginia) and James Wilson (of Pennsylvania), proposed two houses of Congress. Voters—limited to free men—would directly elect the members of the House, which would then choose the members of the Senate from slates proposed by the states. The national legislature (both houses would have members proportional to each state's population) would choose the president and the federal judiciary. The scheme, as Madison saw it, amounted to a "policy of refining the popular appointments by successive filtrations," noted political science educator and author David Brian Robertson in the *American Political Science Review*. A competing so-called New Jersey Plan, pushed by New Jersey delegate William Paterson, called for a single national legislature with each state having one vote.

Throughout June and early July of 1787, delegates debated the merits of the respective proposals. Madison, who had expected an easy victory, was thwarted. As David Brian Robertson pointed out, "Delegates from the economically disadvantaged states that lie between Virginia and Massachusetts composed the core of the opposition to the Virginia Plan. They mobilized against the coalition of six large and southern states that Madison expected to unite behind his initial agenda." Roger Sherman (the mayor of New Haven, who would go on to become a congressman and, ultimately, a senator) was particularly aggressive in opposing the proportional representation plan. Sherman's core argument, as his grandson, amateur historian and US senator George Frisbie

Hoar, put it, was that "each State ought to be able to protect itself, otherwise a few large States will rule the rest."

Sherman's objections were not just to Madison's vision of the Senate. It was, David Brian Robertson added, "only a part of a broader defense of state agency in national policy-making. At every turn, Sherman pressed to enlarge the state legislatures' influence over national policy-makers. He questioned the need for direct election of the House, selection of the Senate by the House, presidential veto power, creation of inferior national courts, and bypassing of state legislatures to ratify the Constitution. He insisted that the national executive be 'absolutely dependent' on Congress. When Madison ally James Wilson warned that state officials, the principal 'losers of power,' were the chief obstacles to popular control of Congress, Sherman portrayed his opponents' position as radical."

The Great Compromise, credited to Sherman as well as fellow Connecticut delegate Oliver Ellsworth, envisioned a two-house national legislature in which "the proportion of suffrage in the first branch . . . should be according to the respective numbers of free inhabitants; and that in the second branch, or Senate, each State should have one vote and no more," as summed up by author Thomas Eddlem.

The proposal, which was initially rejected, passed the convention by a one-vote margin on July 16 (and incorporated the so-called three-fifths clause, allocating additional representation to slave owners). The Great Compromise, in short, passed "by the most narrow margin possible," scholars Jeremy C. Pope and Shawn Treier pointed out. "Had

Massachusetts not voted 'divided,' or had North Carolina not switched sides, the proposal would have failed."

A few days later, on July 23, 1787, delegates agreed to the formula granting each state two senators—as opposed to one or three. The Founders' work did not end with establishing a two-senators-per-state formula. They also made that formula extremely difficult to change. Paul Finkelman in the *University of Chicago Law Review* argued, "The imbecility of the Senate that denies fair political representation to the majority of Americans is compounded by Article V, which provides that 'no State, without its Consent, shall be deprived of its equal Suffrage in the Senate.'"

In his book *How Democratic Is the American Constitution?*, political scientist Robert Dahl suggests that the very notion of providing special rights or protections to smaller states is likely flawed. He finds it unlikely that residents of smaller states possess additional rights or interests that are entitled to protection beyond those enjoyed by residents of large states. Surely, small state dwellers don't have some special right to graze livestock in national parks or "extract minerals from public lands" on favorable terms. Why, wonders Dahl, should "geographical location" privilege one group of citizens over another?

At the Constitutional Convention, he points out, James Wilson asked for whom the national government was being formed: "'Is it for men, or for the imaginary beings called *States*?' Madison was equally dubious about the need to protect the interests of people in the small states. 'Experience,' he said, 'suggests no such danger . . . . Experience rather taught a contrary lesson . . . . The states were divided into different interests not by their differences in size, but by other circumstances.'"

In addition to its other faults, the Great Compromise probably prolonged the institution of slavery, argues Dahl: "Until the 1850s equal representation in the Senate, as [political scientist] Barry Weingast has pointed out, gave 'the South a veto over any policy affecting slavery.' Between 1800 and 1860 eight anti-slavery measures passed the House, and all were killed in the Senate."

Thanks to the Great Compromise, the explosive growth in population differences among states has made America a country where fewer and fewer citizens have a voice. We tolerate that because our Constitution tells us to. Part of the problem, it seems, is that our Constitution is just too damn difficult to amend. Perhaps we need a constitutional amendment to change that. But that, too, is a discussion for another time.

In 1964, the Supreme Court acknowledged (voting 8–1) that something is wrong with a democracy in which some citizens' votes are worth more than others. The case, *Reynolds v. Sims*, had to do with the relative density of voting districts, with whether state senate districts consisting of a few hundred people should be allowed the same representation as districts consisting of thousands or tens of thousands.

In a decision authored by Chief Justice Earl Warren, the Supreme Court declared:

> Legislators represent people, not trees or acres.
> Legislators are elected by voters, not farms or cities or

> economic interests. As long as ours is a representative form of government, and our legislatures are those instruments of government elected directly by and directly representative of the people, the right to elect legislators in a free and unimpaired fashion is a bedrock of our political system. . . . And, if a State should provide that the votes of citizens in one part of the State should be given two times, or five times, or 10 times the weight of votes of citizens in another part of the State, it could hardly be contended that the right to vote of those residing in the disfavored areas had not been effectively diluted. It would appear extraordinary to suggest that a State could be constitutionally permitted to enact a law providing that certain of the State's voters could vote two, five, or 10 times for their legislative representatives, while voters living elsewhere could vote only once. And it is inconceivable that a state law to the effect that, in counting votes for legislators, the votes of citizens in one part of the State would be multiplied by two, five, or 10, while the votes of persons in another area would be counted only at face value, could be constitutionally sustainable.

That decision, of course, did not affect the US Senate, which was mandated by the Constitution to violate the very "one person, one vote" principle the Warren Court overwhelmingly held sacred.

With one huge exception, the rules for electing senators have remained unchanged since the Constitution's ratification. That one big change came over a hundred years ago, when the US decided that ordinary people were finally ready to elect senators directly as opposed to relying on state legislatures to choose them.

In April 1911, by a vote of 166–33, the House adopted a resolution proposing an amendment for the direct election of US senators. The proposal had been defeated in the previous Congress because the so-called Sutherland Amendment (authored by Utah Republican senator George Sutherland) would have given the federal government the right to control federal elections—and therefore, to the horror of southern politicians, might have indirectly given blacks the vote. The *Baltimore Sun* editorialized against Sutherland's gambit, arguing, "This was not proposed as a serious attempt to test the constitutionality of these laws, but was merely a device to force Southern Senators to vote against the resolution for direct election."

The measure was also amended—this time by Kansas Republican senator Joseph Bristow—to provide for a degree of federal supervision. The new bill, which passed the Senate in May 1912, mandated that the "times, places and manner of holding elections for senators and representatives shall be prescribed in each state by the legislatures thereof, but the congress may at any time by law make or alter such regulations, except as to the places of choosing senators." The controversial Senate revision was accepted by the House, despite the grumbling of southern legislators. On May 13 the House passed the measure by a vote of 237–39.

That next morning, the *Atlanta Constitution* reported,

"Since the first resolution for direct election of senators was introduced in 1826 the house has five times passed such a resolution, but the senate has never yet come to terms with the house." Finally, the May 13 vote moved the measure to the states.

On April 8, 1913, the Connecticut legislature became the thirty-sixth state to approve the resolution, ensuring its enactment as the Seventeenth Amendment.

Secretary of State William Jennings Bryan used four pens to formally sign the amendment—one for William, another for Jennings, another for Bryan, and the fourth for the date. "I am sincerely glad that the amendment has been ratified so promptly," declared President Woodrow Wilson, "and a reform so long fought for is at last accomplished."

William E. Borah, a Republican from Idaho who had introduced the resolution in the Senate, predicted, "It will do away with deadlocks and scandals in State Legislatures, and will remove the corrupting influences that have done so much to destroy the confidence of people in the Legislatures. It is safe to say that nine-tenths of the corruption engendered in State Legislatures has its sources in senatorial elections."

• • •

The amendment giving ordinary people—if they were white males—the vote was the last major change in the way senators were elected, unless you include the extension of the vote to nonwhites and women. (General suffrage for women was granted in 1920, with the ratification of the Nineteenth

Amendment. Although blacks were theoretically given the vote by the Fifteenth Amendment following the Civil War, African Americans were not allowed, for the most part, to vote in the South until after passage of the Voting Rights Act in 1965.)

Granted, every now and again someone prominent makes noises about changing the system. Attorney Misha Tseytlin wrote in the *Georgetown Law Journal* in 2006, "While grumblings from large-state representatives like New York's late Senator Daniel Patrick Moynihan that 'sometime in the next century the United States is going to have to address the question of apportionment in the Senate' remain faint, there must be some breaking point at which Americans will begin to question seriously whether the Senate should be reformed."

"If we really want to make progress and achieve greater fairness as a society," argued political scientist Larry Sabato in 2007, "it is time for elemental change. And we should start by looking at the Constitution, with the goal of holding a new Constitutional Convention. . . . But today, the structure of the upper chamber of Congress is completely outmoded. Let's build a fairer Senate by granting the 10 states with the greatest population two additional senators each, and the next 15 most populated states one additional senator each."

In 2019, Eric W. Orts, writing in the *American University Law Review*, put forth what he called the Senate Reform Act. The proposed act, as he described it, "mandates a minimum of one senator for each state. It departs from the original one state, two senators rule, however, and allocates more senators to more populous states, following the constitutional principle of equal voting rights . . . [and] recognizes the legitimacy of representation of the states as independent units within the larger federal system, but rebalances the relative weight given to citizens within these units."

Orts's scheme, well reasoned and moderate as it is, has about as much chance of being enacted as I do of being crowned king of England.

When it comes to changing what is clearly a cockamamie and deeply flawed system, Americans apparently stand helpless—in large measure because we have convinced ourselves that the system has more merit that it has, which no doubt stems from our view of the Founding Fathers—not as flawed mortals who gave as us the tools to improve on their work but as gods who constructed a template for a Perfect Union.

We forget that the Constitution was forged in an era totally unlike our own by frustrated and exhausted men fretting over how to make workable compromises with people who believed in their right to enslave other people, or who just didn't much believe in federal power at all. Somehow the Founders managed, by a one-vote margin, to agree on a scheme for a Senate that defied the very concept of democracy but would allow them to move on.

No one who believes in democracy would come up with such a system today. No one would argue, with a straight face, that the rights of the few outweigh the rights of the many. Imagine, for a second, what would happen if politicians were to propose that we reallocate votes in such a way that every city dweller gets one vote, every suburbanite gets two, and every rural resident gets three. Those politicians would be laughed out of office. Yet we accept, without much question, rules that make the Senate even more inequitable and extreme.

• • •

Allow me to propose this: if the prospect of changing the Constitution is too daunting to contemplate, let's just change the composition of the states.

Imagine what would happen if, say, thirty million people who are black, brown, or under the age of the thirty-five and who now live in megacities, such as New York, Los Angeles, and Chicago, suddenly moved to Wyoming and North Dakota.

Indeed, if we strongly incentivized just three million people of color from the five most populous states (total population: 122,756,000) to relocate to the five least populous (total population: 3,589,000), the political implications would be staggering. Or imagine moving five million voters from the ten most populous states (total population: 177,237,000) to the ten least populous (total population: 9,365,439). The results would be revolutionary. The shift in voting would fundamentally change the US, making it endlessly more democratic. The result would be a significantly healthier and less polarized society.

What would happen if our major foundations decided one part of their mission was actually to form a more perfect union, to make political leadership more representative of the country's citizens? *(Are you listening Gates, Ford, Melon,*

Getty, Johnson, Hewlett, Kellogg, Lilly, Packard, MacArthur, Open Society?) What if, in short, civil society got behind the idea of a New Great Migration? What if major foundations decided to help deserving people of color who were having a hard time in such places as Philadelphia and Washington, DC, and subsidized them and set them up with homes and jobs in, say, New Hampshire and Montana?

Between the early part of the twentieth century and the 1970s an estimated six million African Americans relocated to what they hoped would be more welcoming environments. They left the South, where they could be lynched and brutalized without reason or recourse, where they could be deprived of land, property, and dignity on virtually any random white person's whim, to go in search of somewhere more promising. And they were cheered on by the black press, which made it a mission to give suffering black Southerners hope.

Prominent among the cheerleading newspapers was the *Chicago Defender,* founded by Robert Abbott. As the *Defender* noted on its hundredth anniversary in 2005, "By the advent of World War I, [the *Defender*] was the nation's most influential Black newspaper. Single-handedly, Abbott and the *Defender* set in motion 'The Great Migration.' Abbott kicked-off his Great Northern Drive on May 15, 1917, much to the chagrin of Southern employers. By 1918, over 110,000 people had migrated to Chicago, nearly tripling the city's African-American population."

In *Journalism History*, communications professor Brian Thornton wrote, "The *Defender* played a major role in influencing the Great Migration of African Americans from the rural South to the urban North from roughly 1915 to 1925. That's partly because the *Defender*'s founder and first editor, Robert S. Abbott, wrote many editorials urging African American Southerners to flee the South and head North, 'where there is more humanity, some justice and fairness.' He also posted jobs available in Chicago, described working conditions there as being better than in the South, and even arranged for cheap one-way train fares for those wishing to leave the South."

Today, the black press, like the press in general in the US, has fallen on rather hard times. But civil society is vibrant and thriving. Consider what would happen if it were to take on the mission of saving our endangered democracy?

If we are stuck with polarized voting blocs, let's at least spread them around. Let's find ways to make a virtue out of what has heretofore been a prescription for gridlock and heartbreak—and what has facilitated the imposition of the will of a minority on a helpless majority.

If we lack the determination, the sense, and the power to change the Constitution, we can at least lessen the impact of one of the Founders' biggest mistakes: their acceptance of an obscene distortion of democracy. That situation will only get worse as urban centers continue to grow and our political leaders become increasingly less representative of the country's reality. It's long past time for people of goodwill to change the United States for the better.

7

FLIRTING WITH TYRANNY

During his Memorial Day address, the year before the US entered World War I, President Woodrow Wilson urged young men to volunteer for military service. He also warned immigrants to put our country first. "We have no criticism for men who love the places of their birth and the sources of their origin. . . . But . . . America must come first in every purpose we entertain and every man must count upon being cast out of our confidence, cast out even of our tolerance, who does not submit to the great ruling principle. . . . We are ready to fight against any aggression, whether from within or without."

Wilson's message was clear. If your judgment was so bad, or your allegiance to the country so weak, that you spoke out against the US fighting foreign aggression, you deserved the country's scorn—and had earned deportation, a jail sentence, or both.

A year later, President Wilson requested a congressional declaration of war. That same day, April 2, Washington was besieged by pacifists protesting under the leadership of a group calling itself the Emergency Peace Federation.

The group was jeered, and fights broke out. "There were various disorders," reported the *Baltimore Sun*, "the most sensational incident of the day following a call at the office of Senator [Henry Cabot] Lodge, the veteran legislator from Massachusetts, by a pacifist group from his State. . . . There were harsh words and then blows were exchanged. Senator Lodge sent his antagonist to the floor with a blow to the jaw, and while the office force was clearing away the other pacifists, a young man in the corridor pummeled [a protestor] vigorously before turning him over for a beating at the hands of . . . a half-grown telegraph messenger."

The US declared war not just on Germany and the other Axis powers but also on domestic critics of the war effort—especially those of foreign birth or considered in thrall to foreign ideas. "First Amendment be damned!" became de facto US policy. In official eyes, and in the eyes of much of the public, you were either for the troops—and supportive of the battles they were waging—or an enemy of the state.

That June, Congress passed the Espionage Act of 1917, which prohibited interference of any conceivable sort and many forms of speaking out against the war mobilization. Congress followed that up, in October, with the Trading with the Enemy Act, which made it illegal to transport, carry, publish, or distribute any matter that was "nonmailable" under the Espionage Act.

Postmaster General Albert Sidney Burleson, in a letter to publishers, explained that nonmailable material included statements urging "resistance" to any US laws, or aimed at obstructing recruitment or enlistment, or intending to cause insubordination or disloyalty. Also forbidden were false statements intended to promote the success of enemies and a wide variety of other ideas presumed to be hostile to US interests. Socialist publications would be forbidden, promised Burleson, only if they contained treasonable or seditious matter. "The trouble," he added, "is that most Socialist papers do contain this matter."

The already harsh laws were augmented with passage of the Sedition Act of 1918, which amended the Espionage Act. It made a wide variety of acts and statements illegal, including willfully uttering, printing, writing, or publishing "any language intended to incite, provoke, or encourage resistance to the United States, or to promote the cause of its enemies"; the display of "the flag of any foreign enemy"; and the publication or utterance of anything intended to "cripple or hinder the United States in the prosecution of the war."

Only Representative Meyer London, a socialist from New York, voted against the conference report on the final version of the bill. As the *New York Herald Tribune* reported, "Representative London sought vainly to send the report back to conference because of the elimination of the Senate amendment exempting from penalty those who, in criticism of the government, speak the truth with good motives and for justifiable ends. Representative [William] Gordon, of Ohio, Democrat, declared [that] the Senate placed language in the bill 'which plainly is in violation of the Federal Constitution guaranteeing free speech.'"

The legislation imperiled anyone who for any reason spoke up against, or wrote in opposition to, the war. Eventually, the wartime measures claimed thousands of arguably innocent victims. Among its most notable targets was union activist and perennial socialist presidential candidate Eugene Debs. During a speech in Canton, Ohio, in June 1918, Debs said he had "come to realize . . . that it is extremely dangerous to exercise the constitutional right of free speech in a country fighting to make democracy safe in the world."

Debs went on to attack the war itself: "Every solitary one of these aristocratic conspirators and would-be murderers claims to be an arch-patriot. Every one of them insists that the war is being waged to make the world safe for democracy. What humbug! What rot! What false pretense! These autocrats, these tyrants, these red-handed robbers and murderers" call themselves patriots "while the men who have the courage to stand face to face with them, speak the truth, and fight for their exploited victims . . . are [considered] disloyalists and traitors."

Debs criticized the government's treatment of Kate Richards O'Hare, a socialist, segregationist, and former congressional candidate from Kansas who had been sentenced to five years in prison for giving a speech in Bowman, North Dakota, in which she said American women who raised sons for the army were "no better than brood sows."

For that speech, Debs was charged with four counts of violating the Espionage Act. The outspoken socialist refused to make a legal defense during his widely covered trial in Cleveland. Instead, he told the jury, "I have no dispute with the evidence presented by the Government, no criticism for the counsel for the prosecution. I would not take back a word of what I believe right to save myself from the penitentiary. I am accused of crime; but I look the court in the face. I look the jury in the face. I look the world in the face, for in my heart, no accusation of wrong festers." He added, "I deny nothing. I repudiate nothing. I retract nothing."

Debs was found guilty on three counts: inciting insubordination and disloyalty; uttering language tending to incite resistance to the United States; and promoting the enemy's cause. He was sentenced to ten years in prison.

Perhaps the most bizarre prosecution was of Robert Goldstein, a moviemaker. Goldstein's debut film, *The Spirit of '76*, premiered in May 1917—the month following the United States' entry into the war. It was intended as a patriotic celebration of the country's victory in the Revolutionary War. Unfortunately for Goldstein, Great Britain was now a US ally, which brought the movie under the sway of the Espionage Act. Federal officials were disturbed by a scene that depicted British soldiers bayoneting women and children during the Wyoming Valley Massacre.

Goldstein appeared before federal judge Benjamin Bledsoe in Los Angeles in November 1917 after his movie had been confiscated. The judge pointed out that Goldstein had been warned that "the bayoneting of the babe and the like . . . had been severely criticized and were inhibited." Bledsoe added:

> At the present time . . . the United States is confronted with what I conceive to be the greatest emergency we have ever been confronted with at any time in our history. There is now required of us the greatest amount of devotion to a common cause, the greatest amount of co-operation, the greatest amount of efficiency, and the greatest amount of disposition to further the ultimate success of American arms that can be conceived, and as a necessary consequence no man should be permitted, by deliberate act, or even unthinkingly, to do that which will in any way detract from the efforts which the United States is putting forth or serve to postpone for a single moment the early coming of the day when the success of our arms shall be a fact and the righteousness of our cause shall have been demonstrated.

Bledsoe also pointed out that "history is history, and fact is fact. There is no doubt about that," but "this is no time" for "those things that may have the tendency . . . of creating animosity or want of confidence between us and our allies."

That December, Goldstein was charged with three counts of violating the Espionage Act. He was accused of attempting to arouse antagonism against an ally, discouraging registration for military service, and conspiring to discourage registration. The following May, he was convicted and sentenced by Bledsoe to ten years in prison and fined $5,000.

The Ninth Circuit Court of Appeals upheld his conviction that October.

• • •

The most high-profile prosecution under the Espionage Act was of the Industrial Workers of the World—the union otherwise referred to as the Wobblies. Even before the US entered the war, federal and local government officials were fed up with the union's militant opposition to industry's leadership and its blatant socialist leanings.

In November 1916, an estimated 250 IWW members had come from Seattle aboard a steamer to support striking shingle workers in Everett, Washington. The local sheriff, backed by big business interests and an armed posse of two hundred, refused to allow the unionists to disembark. Shots were fired, and seven people ended up dead (five IWW members and two deputies). Some seventy-four IWW members were held for trial. Following a nine-week trial, local IWW leader Thomas Tracy was acquitted of a deputy sheriff's murder. The other IWW members were eventually released without trial; but the IWW's travails were far from over.

In March 1917, IWW founding member and general-secretary William "Big Bill" Haywood gave an interview to the *Christian Science Monitor* in which he held forth on the IWW mission: "The working class and the employing class have nothing in common. There can be no peace so long as hunger and want are found among millions of working people, and the few who make up the employing class have all the good things of life. Between these two classes a struggle must go on until the workers of the world organize as a class, take possession of the earth and the machinery of production, and abolish the wage system. What the IWW seeks . . . is an industrial democracy, in which every man is a worker."

Such sentiments led to widespread revulsion among industrial leaders and politicians, such as Senator Charles Thomas of Ohio, who denounced the IWW as a group of anarchists, aligned with the country's enemies.

The new laws gave the IWW's many opponents a formidable weapon.

In September 1917, the Justice Department raided IWW offices around the country, arresting much of the leadership and confiscating thousands of documents. The *New York Herald Tribune* reported in an article datelined from Washington, "On orders from Attorney General [Thomas Watt] Gregory, United States marshals in many towns and cities descended at 2 p.m. central time upon local headquarters of the Industrial Workers of the World, seized books, checks, correspondence and other documents, and, in some instances, arrested officials found on the premises."

Among the crimes charged were publishing seditious articles and sabotaging machinery. The Justice Department made a series of other claims concerning German spies and plans to destroy wheat and corn crops. Citing no evidence, the *New York Times* reported, "Sabotage and fire were to have been the principal weapons of the IWW in the destruction of a considerable part of the food supply of the United States and the Allies." None of those things ever came close to being proved.

Nonetheless, the Justice Department followed up the raids with indictments of some 166 IWW members for involvement in a seditious conspiracy against the government. The Justice Department declared, "Boiled down and stated in a few words, the propaganda of these defendants consists of these assertions: 'We are going to take possession of the industries of this country.' . . . In addition, there is running through all those endeavors a pronounced opposition to the support of the war in which this country is enlisted, the teaching being that whatever can be done to make the power of the enemy greater or our power of resistance least effective is a service to the organization."

The indictments resulted in the biggest trial—conducted in federal court in Chicago—the US had ever seen. The trial, which began April 1, 1918, was presided over by federal judge Kenesaw Mountain Landis. At that point (following the dropping of various charges and the disappearance of various targeted individuals), the number of defendants had decreased. Some 112 of the 113 charged showed up in the Chicago courtroom and pronounced themselves innocent before jury selection began.

During his opening remarks on May 2, Special Prosecutor Frank Nebeker promised to prove a vast conspiracy: "This campaign reached out over the entire country and appealed to certain people who did not want to see America enter the conflict for various reasons. The leaders of this anti-war campaign took the attitude that should America lose the war the ultimate result would not be contrary to their aims. . . . Therefore, they called strikes to break down

America's munition production plans. They urged violation of the selective draft act; they called our soldiers 'yellow legs.'"

Throughout the trial little evidence of actual wrongdoing was introduced. Instead, the prosecution presented inflammatory statements, pamphlets advocating "sabotage" that were never approved by the union leadership, and even read into the record a description of a "vision" that had come to a defendant named Harrison George of the IWW rising up as saviors while President Wilson and his cabinet fled.

On April 17, 1918, the last day of the proceedings, Prosecutor Nebeker told jurors they had "engaged in one of the most epoch-making trials in the history of this country." Although charges against several of those arrested were dismissed during the trial, it took the jury took less than an hour to find all remaining 101 defendants guilty.

Union leader Haywood was shocked. "I can't understand how some of us were not acquitted at a moment's notice," he said. "I rather looked for a hung jury on some of us, but that all should be convicted so quickly is the surprise of my life."

The *St. Louis Post-Dispatch* was one of the many newspapers that celebrated the outcome: "Law reigns and under its protecting rule our free Government will work out the will of the people in war and peace and demonstrate the soundness of the principles upon which the republic is founded. The imported methods of European anarchists, nourished by despotism, caste and class privilege, fail in free America."

Haywood and his fourteen chief aides received the maximum of twenty years in prison and were fined $20,000. The other defendants were sentenced to periods ranging from ten days to ten years, with fines of $5,000. Before imposing sentence, Judge Landis lectured the group: "In times of peace you have a legal right to oppose, by free speech, preparations for war. But when war has been declared that right ceases forthwith."

• • •

In November 1918 the war ended, only to be followed by the Red Scare, during which thousands in the US were arrested and otherwise persecuted, particularly during the so-called Palmer Raids (named for Attorney General A. Mitchell Palmer). But eventually the hysteria died down.

Hundreds of those charged under the wartime laws were pardoned or had their sentences commuted to time served. It was not until 1952 (*Joseph Burstyn, Inc. v. Wilson*) that the Supreme Court granted films protection under the First Amendment, which was a few decades too late for Goldstein, whose sentence nonetheless had been commuted after three years and who died in obscurity.

That period—World War I and its immediate aftermath—was the lowest point in modern times for civil liberties in the US. But it was not the only low point. Although we learned during that era that we abandon the Bill of Rights at our own peril, we continued to do so—to varying degrees and with various groups—whenever we felt threatened.

We interned more than a hundred thousand persons of Japanese American extraction during World War II, though we knew enough not to resurrect the Sedition Act and start deporting foreigners wholesale. And we made all manner of bad calls during the early phases of the Cold War. We allowed Senator Joseph McCarthy to become a one-man civil liberties wrecking crew. And we empowered the House Un-American Activities Committee (of "Are you now or have you ever been" fame) to ruin lives across the country—particularly the lives of those in the arts, and especially Jews—simply for being suspected of viewing the world differently from the zealots demanding their scalps.

Even once those embarrassing episodes were behind us, we could not extinguish our impulse to equate repression with safety. As legal scholar Erwin Chemerinsky put it, "For over 200 years, repression has been the response to threats to security. In hindsight, every such instance was clearly a grave error that restricted our most precious freedoms for no apparent gain."

The almost instinctive reaction—the impulse to crush dissent at times when the nation seems endangered—will probably always be with us. It certainly governed our response to the tragedy of 9/11. Legal scholar Samuel Walker argues that President George W. Bush had "the worst record of any president" on civil liberties issues. "The USA PATRIOT Act is packed with threats to freedom of speech and due process protections. His administration has justified holding people indefinitely without charges, and in a broader sense it has made sweeping claims that it is not bound by legal precedents or existing human rights standards."

Barack Obama continued many of the anti-terrorism policies of the Bush administration. After Obama acknowledged he was considering using military tribunals to try 9/11 defendants, the ACLU became so fed up that it ran full-page ads picturing Obama morphing into George Bush. Edward Snowden's realization that Obama's people were continuing Bush's secret mass surveillance programs was, in large measure, his reason for becoming a whistleblower.

The takeaway, it seems, is that regardless of a leader's ideological leanings or party affiliations, we, as a nation, should always be prepared to see our leader turn to repression of dissent and speech as a solution to imminent apparent danger.

• • •

Does that mean Donald Trump is no different from those who have come before him?

Not exactly. Donald Trump represents an entirely new level of threat to civil liberties and the culture of civilized discourse—and not just because he loves to call the press the "enemy of the people."

Prior to his election, Trump made clear that he had little stomach for free speech. During a rally in Fort Worth, Texas, in February 2016, Trump talked up his desire to "open up our libel laws so when they write purposely negative and horrible and false articles, we can sue them and win lots of money."

It was widely assumed that President Trump might mount a frontal attack on the country's free speech rights, but he apparently concluded early on that he had no power to revoke the First Amendment. Still, from day one he vigorously attacked the press, finally—in solidarity with dictators around the world—settling on labeling it the "enemy of the people." And after numerous threats, Trump had his campaign office sue CNN, *The Washington Post*, and the *New York Times* for opinion pieces that angered him.

Virtually no one outside Trump's orbit gave the lawsuits any chance of success. *The Wall Street Journal* observed, "The Trump campaign's defamation claims against the *New York Times* on Feb. 26, the *Post* on Monday and CNN on Friday appear to be unprecedented, legal scholars said. Courts have heard defamation lawsuits from governors, an ex-president and a presidential candidate, but legal scholars said they couldn't recall the last time a sitting U.S. president or his campaign elevated grievances against the news media into civil legal action."

Suing newspapers was not Trump's only unorthodox behavior. Unable to deliver a fatal blow to America's free press, Trump instead focused largely on simply creating an alternative reality, one that would allow him—despite the press's efforts to keep him honest—to justify his attempts to make life hell for whatever group he wanted to target, while rendering the press largely irrelevant as a check on his repressive impulses.

In the past, when presidents have wanted to attack civil liberties or restrict the rights of groups, they have pointed to some unifying threat—generally a war. World War I, World War II, the attack of 9/11 all provided a rationale for cracking down on dissent. But despite assorted global military conflicts Trump inherited from Obama, Trump had no major war or foreign enemy against whom he could rally the nation. So he opted to manufacture threats—the equivalent of a wartime adversary—against which his partisans could unite.

Long before he became president, Trump was practiced at polarizing people by manufacturing divisive threats and targeting innocent objects of scorn. In 1989, years before he set his mind on becoming president, after five black and Latino teens were charged with a horrendous sexual assault, Trump took out full-page ads in several New York newspapers urging readers to "send a message loud and clear to those who would murder our citizens and terrorize New York—BRING BACK THE DEATH PENALTY AND BRING BACK OUR POLICE!"

The ad did not explicitly say the young men were guilty—they had not yet been tried, much less convicted, as his lawyers presumably pointed out to Trump—but his implication was clear. These young men constituted the advance guard of a rampaging horde that would devour all decency in New York and they deserved to die. Indeed, years after they had been completely exonerated of any wrongdoing, Trump continued to insist on their guilt.

No one realized it at the time, but Trump was improvising a formula for success through political polarization. The formula requires first that you brand members of some group as threatening and then demonize them for the sake of a fearful yet receptive audience. It did not require much effort from Trump to adapt that formula as he prepared himself for a White House run.

He tested it on June 16, 2015, the day he announced his campaign. "When Mexico sends its people, they're not sending their best. . . . They're sending people that have lots of problems, and they're bringing those problems [to] us. They're bringing drugs. They're bringing crime. They're rapists. And some, I assume, are good people," declared Trump.

Mexico's interior minister Miguel Ángel Osorio Chong quickly responded with "The remarks by Donald Trump seem prejudicial and absurd," and accused Trump of attempting to "generate controversy."

Osorio Chong, of course, was correct. And the remarks did indeed generate controversy, which is simply another word for attention, which Trump deeply coveted. But they also got across how he intended to position himself, as the political equivalent of a great white hope: the fearless warrior who would be the noble shield against the human vermin who, without his intervention, would "pour into and infest our country."

Trump would make his courageous stand at the border. He would fight and win the United States' last war—against illegitimate dark people and the Democratic Party that would defend them. Having created the war—if only a metaphorical one—Trump was free to draw on the tools of the repression handbook, which in this case included ripping children from their mothers' arms and putting them in cages, and banning Muslims from countries he abhorred.

Trump discovered, with his big lie about the Central Park Five and even bigger lie about Barack Obama being a native of Kenya, that outrageous, often-repeated lies have a way of trumping truth, and ultimately of undermining reality. Who needs to ban the press when you can simply talk over it—better yet, force it to endlessly repeat the lies you spew? Even if they try to fact-check a portion of those lies, the press will still serve them up to the public, an appreciable percentage of which will believe the president over the journalists.

In October 2019, *The Washington Post* reported that, after nearly 1,000 days as president, Donald Trump was telling lies at an accelerating pace. "As of Oct. 9, his 993rd day in office, he had made 13,435 false or misleading claims, according to the Fact Checker's database that analyzes, categorizes and tracks every suspect statement he has uttered. That's an average of almost 22 claims a day since our last update 65 days ago."

Comedians have made fortunes lampooning the president's propensity to lie. And it certainly has created hilarious moments. But in the end, it is not a joking matter.

Trump has demonized workers in the FBI and the Justice Department. And he has taken a blowtorch to the intelligence agencies charged with insulating us from foreign deceits and manipulation—even firing his acting director of intelligence for allowing a subordinate to tell Congress that Russian hackers were working to reelect Trump. "In other words," as *TIME* magazine summed it up, "Trump is objecting not to the facts his top intelligence experts are presenting, but to the truth they reveal."

To make matters worse, Trump has coarsened, perhaps irremediably, the quality of public debate. Instead of engaging opponents on the merits of their arguments, he denounces them as short and fat, or low IQ, or shifty, low energy, pathetic, crazed, radical, unqualified, weak, losers, and the list goes on and on, with never a serious thought or argument offered in evidence.

In an op-ed published in *The Washington Post* in December 2019, former UN ambassador and former South Carolina governor Nikki Haley argued that it would be much more difficult to remove the confederate flag from the South Carolina statehouse today than it was in 2015 (which she did following Dylann Roof's racially motivated church murders). "The reason is not the upsurge in white nationalism. While that is a very disturbing trend that must be resisted, it has not changed the composition of the South Carolina legislature that needed a two-thirds vote to remove the flag. Rather, the reason is today's media hysteria that makes it far more difficult to have the kind of thoughtful and prayerful dialogue we had following the Charleston murders." Haley blames an "outrage culture," a poisonous atmosphere generated by misguided liberals who insist on labeling defenders of the confederate flag as racists.

Haley somehow manages to ignore that the biggest proponent of outrage culture happens to be her former boss in the White House, who, it turns out, is a hero to the very white nationalists across the globe whom she believes are "disturbing."

If Haley were interested in making a serious argument about outrage culture, she would begin with the Outrager in Chief. But she does not have the courage to do that. She has political options to maintain, a possible presidential candidacy to protect, and she cannot do that and stand up to the bully in the White House.

Having made himself into the champion white warrior who is fending off the rampaging, unwashed minority horde from hellholes at home and abroad, Trump has united a formidable army behind him. And many of his enlistees make up the core of the modern Republican Party. That reality—

combined with the power of technology, specifically the technology of tweets—has given Trump unprecedented sway over his party leadership and made a joke of the very idea of checks and balances and division of power.

That virtually unchecked power enables him to commit impeachable offenses with near impunity, and to sneer at those who would keep him in line. This is not really what the Founders had in mind. They never believed political parties would become so dominant, that national politicians would become so craven, or that someone like Donald Trump—who cares not a whit about precedent, propriety, deference, the rights of others, or honest communication—would ever occupy the presidency. The Electoral College, after all, was supposed to see to it that no person lacking character ever got near the White House. But the Founders could not have foreseen how inadequate their supposed safeguards would be when tested by an unimagined future.

8

STRIDENT STUDENTS AND SILENCED VOTERS

Over the past few years, the US has been experiencing a full-blown free-speech crisis, emanating largely from its more liberal college campuses. Students are willy-nilly shouting down speakers, wrecking professors' lives, and rooting out politically incorrect discourse—especially from the Right. Or so we are told—and provided with seemingly countless examples.

The problem goes back to at least 2015, when outraged black students at Emory University complained of various incidents and perceived slights. They urged the university to explore, via faculty evaluations, the problem of professors perpetrating harmful "microaggressions" on vulnerable minorities. They also demanded that the university "geofence," or block, a social media app that allowed users to gossip anonymously and to spread "intolerable and psychologically detrimental" rumors and opinions.

The student newspaper ran a piece accusing the black students of demanding censorship, and a university work group recommended against blocking the app.

Nonetheless, students at other campuses demanded that the Yik Yak app (which eventually went out of business) be prohibited. In early 2016, a commission at the University of Rochester recommended that the university block the app. President Joel Seligman rejected the recommendation, arguing that trying to block it not only would be ineffectual but could undercut "the free expression rights of our faculty members, the student newspaper, speaker selection," and faculty hiring. A small group of private colleges did ban the app but found that students could access it anyway.

Meanwhile, students at Northwestern University's School of Communication created a brouhaha by demanding action against a professor deemed insensitive to improper sexual behavior. The professor, Laura Kipnis, set off the tempest by publishing an article entitled "Sexual Paranoia Strikes Academe" in *The Chronicle of Higher Education*.

"When I was in college, hooking up with professors was more or less part of the curriculum," wrote Kipnis, who poked fun at the current climate. She also took aim at "new campus codes." Those codes, in her telling, have people "kowtowing to the fiction" that professors are all-powerful. "If this is feminism, it's feminism hijacked by melodrama," she observed. She wrote about a colleague charged with Title IX, or sex discrimination, violations after an evening out with a student. The experience ended in conflicting stories about being groped. Kipnis cited that professor's ordeal as an example of how "in the post-Title IX landscape, sexual panic rules. Slippery slopes abound. Gropers become rapists and accusers become survivors."

Students demanded that the university punish Kipnis for sharing that opinion. Subsequently, two students lodged Title IX complaints against her. According to *The Washington Post*, "Kipnis wasn't allowed to have an attorney with her for her meeting with investigators; she wasn't apprised of her charges before the meeting; she had to fight with the investigators over recording the session."

"I'd plummeted into an underground world of secret tribunals and capricious, medieval rules, and I wasn't supposed to tell anyone about it," wrote Kipnis, who was exonerated.

FIRE—the Foundation for Individual Rights in Education, a free speech group—has been tracking university speech codes since 2006. Their research suggests that policies that "clearly and substantially restrict freedom of speech" have declined. In its 2020 report, FIRE noted that 24.2 percent of the 471 colleges and universities surveyed maintained at least one speech policy restrictive enough to earn the organization's "red light," or worst, rating but pointed out, "This is the twelfth year in a row that the percentage of schools earning a red-light rating has gone down; last year, 28.5% of schools earned a red-light rating."

FIRE also claimed, "Though these improvements in policy are heartening, free speech on campus remains under threat. Demands for censorship of student and faculty speech—

whether originating on or off campus—are common, and universities continue to investigate and punish students and faculty over protected expression."

There have been some instances in which protestors on campus went beyond simply attacking speech to interfering with media coverage. In November 2015, Tim Tai, a stringer for ESPN, was covering protests against racial abuse and other alleged problems at the University of Missouri when students blocked his way, physically denying him access to a public space. A young man threatened him with "You better back up." At another point, several students chanted, "Hey, hey, ho, ho, reporters have got to go."

Missouri student Mark Schierbecker, who caught the scene on video, was confronted by Melissa Click, an assistant professor of mass media. Click grabbed his camera and pushed him. "You need to get out," she told him. When Schierbecker refused, she turned to the crowd and asked, "Who wants to help me get this reporter out of here?"

After a public uproar, Click issued a statement apologizing for her behavior, which Schierbecker rejected as insincere.

Demonstrators at Smith College gathered in support of the students at the University of Missouri and generated headlines of their own. They refused to allow reporters to cover their sit-in unless they agreed to "articulate their solidarity" with the students—a demand that most reporters would consider a flagrant violation of press freedom. The university backed the students. "It's a student event, and we respect their right to do that, although it poses problems for the traditional media," explained the university's director of media.

The year 2017 brought the even more high-profile case of Milo Yiannopoulos, a reliably provocative speaker who had worked as a senior editor with Breitbart News. Yiannopoulos was invited to the University of California, Berkeley, that February by a Republican student group. Before he appeared, hundreds of demonstrators showed up on campus, some of them throwing rocks and fireworks. In the commotion, a generator was set afire.

Concerned about safety, the university cancelled the event. Yiannopoulos gleefully denounced the protestors on Facebook: "One thing we do know for sure: The Left is absolutely terrified of free speech and will do literally anything to shut it down."

The cancellation stirred President Trump, who tweeted, "If U.C. Berkeley does not allow free speech and practices violence on innocent people with a different point of view - NO FEDERAL FUNDS?" He followed up the tweet, in March 2019, with an executive order, which essentially insisted that universities follow the law and federal policy. "If a college or university does not allow you to speak, we will not give them money," said Trump.

UC Berkeley School of Law dean Erwin Chemerinsky attributed the violence not to students but to "150 masked agitators" intent on disrupting an otherwise peaceful protest. Campus officials, he insisted, were fully aware of their First Amendment obligations and had even resisted demands to cancel Yiannopoulos's appearance.

In September 2017, Yiannopoulos was again scheduled to speak on campus, as a participant in a "Free Speech Week" that he was involved in organizing. At a press conference prior to his appearance, Yiannopoulos insisted, "We are going to be hosting an event, come hell or high water, tomorrow."

The rally did not live up to expectations. Several announced speakers—including commentator Ann Coulter and former Trump aide Stephen Bannon—never confirmed and did not show. Because it was not an official university event, the university did not supply audio equipment. Yiannopoulos ended up addressing, without amplification, a small crowd of fans and a larger swarm of protestors. "[Thirty] minutes into his arrival, Yiannopoulos fled the area as his security detail escorted him to a white SUV," reported the *Huffington Post*.

"After months of sometimes violent clashes between the far left and far right on the streets of Berkeley," observed the *Los Angeles Times*, "Sunday's event was decidedly anticlimactic—with the air of something hyped being deflated." The *Times* also noted: "The school has incurred at least $1.4 million in security costs since February, when Yiannopoulos' last appearance sparked violent protests. The campus spent $200,000 on security for that event, $600,000 for Coulter, whose event ultimately didn't happen, and an estimated $600,000 for the talk recently by conservative writer Ben Shapiro, according to the university."

A month after Yiannopoulos's disappointingly low-key appearance at UC Berkeley, former congressman Barney Frank and former New Hampshire governor John H. Sununu participated in a public dialogue at Middlebury College. That discussion came several months after protests at Middlebury had thwarted a speech by author Charles Murray, who is best known for arguing that blacks and Latinos are dumber than whites.

Sununu called such disruptions of speakers "the biggest problem in America today."

Frank responded, "I don't think it's the biggest problem in America, but it's outrageous. . . . That's not the way you want a democracy."

Sununu countered, "The reason I think it's the biggest problem, or one of the biggest problems, is because it's producing a generation of young people who are on campus and who will be leaving campus who, in my opinion, are being encouraged by a lot of faculty members to feel that the First Amendment is not an appropriate right in this country. To me, none of the other rights work without First Amendment rights."

Those who see college speech antics in a similarly apocalyptic light took some comfort in fall 2016 when the University of Chicago sent incoming freshmen a letter, from John Ellison, the dean of students, setting limits on what the university would tolerate. The letter invoked the university's commitment to "freedom of inquiry and expression" and its disapproval of censorship. It defended civility, denounced harassment undertaken in the name of free speech, and encouraged students to engage in rigorous discussion and debate—even if that caused discomfort. Given the university's commitment to academic freedom, wrote Ellison, "we do not cancel invited speakers because their topics might prove controversial, and we do not condone the creation of intellectual 'safe spaces' where individuals can retreat from ideas and perspectives at odds with their own."

University of Chicago president Robert Zimmer published an op-ed in *The Wall Street Journal* in which he defended "free expression and the open exchange of ideas." Universities, he declared, "cannot be viewed as a sanctuary for comfort but rather as a crucible for confronting ideas and thereby learning to make informed judgments in complex environments. Having one's assumptions challenged and experiencing the discomfort that sometimes accompanies this process are intrinsic parts of an excellent education."

The conservative *Washington Examiner* heartily applauded the university's initiative in putting "crybullies" in their place: "Until a few years ago, students didn't require safe spaces and trigger warnings, or to be shielded from speakers with whom they disagreed. This is a new phenomenon, and it's why today's students are being described as 'entitled' and 'coddled.'"

The Washington Post noted that students at the University of Chicago were not necessarily thrilled with the university's position. It quoted Eric Holmberg, the student government president, who thought it was "a step backward in addressing the toxic campus climate. It seems the university does not want to engage in those ideas. . . . We have an LGBQT [*sic*] office, they offer safe-space training, they have made an effort to provide safe spaces. Then the dean of students, who's responsible for student life, is saying the university doesn't like safe spaces."

Nonetheless, numerous universities signed on to adhere to the so-called "Chicago principles." And as Bill Lueders, managing editor of *The Progressive*, pointed out in a 2017 article, several colleges already had codes in place allowing students to be disciplined if they obstructed authorized events.

Lee Bollinger, president of Columbia University, penned a piece for *The Atlantic* in June 2019 titled "Free Speech on Campus Is Doing Just Fine, Thank You." The article was motivated in part by Trump's free speech executive order, which Bollinger dismissed as "a transparent exercise in politics. Its intent was to validate the collective antipathy that many Trump boosters feel toward institutions of higher learning."

Bollinger's more substantive point was that speech on college campuses was a perennial work in progress: "The president's claim that the campus free-speech order was needed to defend 'American values that have been under siege' ignored two essential facts. First, universities are, today, more hospitable venues for open debate than the nation as a whole. Second, not only have fierce arguments over where to draw the line on acceptable speech been a familiar occurrence in the United States for the past century, but such dialogue has also been indispensable to building a society that embraces the First Amendment."

His point, in short, was that universities, more than most US institutions, are seriously wrestling with the difficult questions that protection of free speech raises.

The attempt to balance the demands of free speech against other societal values often leaves students, as well as administrators, conflicted and confused. Consequently, students often get things wrong. Disinviting speakers and hijacking events are rude things to do. Such behavior certainly does nothing to promote intelligent dialogue or enhance understanding. And just about any intelligent person would throw up their hands at demands by students to be protected against ideas, facts, and narratives they don't happen to endorse. But as Bollinger insinuated, the recent so-called crisis is driven as much by a cynical conservative agenda as by any fundamental hostility on campuses to free expression.

When conservative groups intentionally invite the most offensive and grating speakers they can find, they are not exactly surprised that certain more progressive classmates take the bait. Indeed, that is what they hope for, since the real objective is to make the "other side" come off as weak, intolerant, troubled "snowflakes."

It also is true that progressive-minded students can do ill-advised or intolerant things all on their own, as when they attack professors for simply expressing views with which they disagree or—as happened at Harvard—when they retaliate against faculty members for standing up for the rights of someone they find loathsome.

At Harvard University in 2019 students agitated for the removal of two faculty deans—law professor Ronald Sullivan and his wife, Stephanie Robinson, a lecturer at Harvard Law—after Sullivan agreed to represent accused serial predator Harvey Weinstein in court.

When Sullivan became part of Weinstein's legal team, some students were surprised and horrified, feeling "his decision to represent a person accused of abusing women disqualified Mr. Sullivan from serving in a role of support and mentorship to students," reported the *New York Times*. A recent graduate complained in *The Harvard Crimson* that Sullivan's decision to represent Weinstein felt "like a personal betrayal." She added, "I don't just disagree with Sullivan's actions; I'm ashamed of them."

In addition to their law school positions, the couple were resident deans—in-house counselors—at Winthrop House, which is essentially a dorm. As the uproar grew, the university responded by ejecting Sullivan and his wife from Winthrop House. The dean of Harvard College released a statement that didn't explain much of anything but took refuge in a sort of institutional gobbledygook. The concerns expressed by students and staff "have been serious and numerous," wrote Dean Rakesh Khurana. "The actions that have been taken to improve the climate have been ineffective, and the noticeable lack of faculty dean presence during critical moments has further deteriorated the climate in the house. I have concluded that the situation in the house is untenable."

Sullivan responded with a *New York Times* op-ed: "I am willing to believe that some students felt unsafe. But feelings alone should not drive university policy." Sullivan accused the university of having "capitulated to protesters" and added, "Given that universities are supposed to be places of considered and civil discourse, where people are forced to wrestle with difficult, controversial and unfamiliar ideas, this is disappointing."

ACLU officials criticized Harvard for sacrificing principle "in an apparent quest for an easy way out."

It was not Harvard's finest hour. But as craven as Harvard's actions appear, and as reactionary as the student demand for reprisals seems to be (given that it shows intolerance of the right of the despised to a defense, which is a bedrock principle of US jurisprudence), such brouhahas do not constitute a national crisis. If anything, they speak to the usefulness of a mandatory seminar at universities on the values of free speech in American society. Also, the so-called campus crisis seems largely self-correcting. There are enough clear and cool heads on universities that sanity often seems to prevail.

• • •

A more serious threat to speech—and certainly to democracy—may have little to do with students' attitudes toward free speech but instead with the inability of most students to competently process information received online. We seem to be witnessing a crisis of critical reasoning and intellectual curiosity so profound that it leaves young people frighteningly vulnerable to the cleverly disguised propaganda and false messaging that have become an inextricable part of communicating in the internet age.

A Stanford University team reported in 2019 on its national assessment of some 3,446 US high school students, specifically on their ability to make sense of information distributed online. "The results—if they can be summarized in a word—are troubling," reported the researchers. "Fifty-two percent of students believed a grainy video claiming to show ballot stuffing in the 2016 Democratic primaries (the video was actually shot in Russia) constituted 'strong evidence' of voter fraud in the U.S. Among more than 3,000 responses, only three students tracked down the source of the video, even though a quick search turns up a variety of articles exposing the ruse."

The results of Stanford's previous research were no less troubling. A variety of tasks assigned to middle school, high school, and college students revealed that many were stunningly incompetent in critically assessing online information. Huge numbers turned out to be extremely bad at distinguishing between information presented in supposedly objective news reports and information presented in commentary or paid postings. Students rarely questioned sources of online information. "Even when given the opportunity in a live web task, students rarely showed evidence of venturing outside the webpage on which they landed. Although they were explicitly instructed that they were free to search outside the site."

The guiding assumption behind the right to free speech is that people hearing that speech—or some reasonable percentage of them—are capable of understanding what it means. What is the point of presenting people with information if they are incapable of digesting it?

Stanford's research suggests, at a minimum, that schools and universities have a huge task in front of them in helping students learn how to critically evaluate the information—and misinformation—flooding helter-skelter into their brains. The health of our democracy depends on us—young and old alike—getting much better than we currently are at that.

It depends also on us getting serious about confronting the myriad challenges to robust political participation that have little to do with online literacy or speech on college campuses. Whatever students may feel about free speech, it is not students who are putting every conceivable obstacle possible in the way of many Americans exercising their right to vote.

• • •

Is voting a form of speech? If so, should voting be given the same protection as speech? In his *Citizens United* dissent, Justice John Paul Stevens made his opinion clear: "Under the majority's view, I suppose it may be a First Amendment problem that corporations are not permitted to vote, given that voting is, among other things, a form of speech."

Civil rights attorneys Armand Derfner and J. Gerald Hebert argued in the *Yale Law & Policy Review* that the Supreme Court should treat voting as a "fundamental right," one that deserves at least as much protection as does the money spent to influence votes: "The court has routinely noted that the right to vote is the right to have a 'voice' in elections and has already acknowledged the First Amendment implications of voter petitions. Therefore, taking the remaining step of ensuring full First Amendment protection for voting itself would be a markedly less dramatic doctrinal shift than remaking another clause of the Constitution."

The court is not likely to do that anytime soon. But let us assume, for the sake of this discussion, that voting is a form of speech worth protecting. It is certainly the ultimate expression of what is arguably the paramount reason for free speech: to ensure democracy's control by an informed electorate.

Yet we stand by, all but helpless, as forces with a distinctly political agenda vigorously move to limit the vote of certain populations. As the *New York Times* pointed out in an April 2018 editorial, "In the years before Mr. Trump's election and in the time since, Republican lawmakers around the country aggressively pushed through laws to make voting harder for certain groups, particularly minorities. Poll taxes and literacy tests have given way to voter-ID laws, cutbacks to early voting and same-day registration, polling place closings, voter-roll purges, racially discriminatory redistricting and felon disenfranchisement laws—most of which, though justified on race-neutral grounds, harm minority voters more."

The challenges faced by Stacey Abrams, in her attempt to become Georgia's (and the United States') first black female governor in 2018, give some insight into what that Republican-orchestrated campaign looks like. Abrams lost that race by less than 55,000 votes to Brian Kemp. There will forever be an asterisk by that result, because in the six years prior to her election, Georgia purged some 1.4 million voters from its rolls. In those years, Kemp, as Georgia's secretary of state, was a primary player in the voter purge from which he evidently benefitted.

The experience so infuriated Abrams that she channeled her energies into organizing Fair Fight 2020, a national voting rights campaign. "I am not convinced at all that we will have free and fair elections unless we work to make it so," she told *The Guardian*. "In America, we have the theory of free and fair elections, but unfortunately we've seen, particularly over the last 20 years, an erosion of the ability to access that right."

In October 2019, Brad Raffensperger, Georgia's new secretary of state, released a list of an additional 313,000 voters he wanted to purge after the targeted voters had not responded to a mailed notice. Despite a suit opposing the action filed by Fair Fight Action, an Abrams initiative, a federal judge ruled in December 2019 that the purge could proceed.

Shortly before that ruling, a judge ordered Wisconsin to jettison some 234,000 voters suspected of having moved to new addresses. The order was in response to a suit filed by the Wisconsin Institute for Law and Liberty, described as a "conservative, libertarian, public interest law firm" by the Center for Media and Democracy's SourceWatch.

"It's no mystery what will happen if Wisconsin's high court sides against the commission," observed journalist Mark Joseph Stern in *Slate*. "An analysis by the *Milwaukee Journal Sentinel* found that residents of Milwaukee and Madison—two of Wisconsin's relatively diverse and heavily Democratic cities—were more likely to be targeted. These individuals account for 14 percent of the state's registered voters but received 23 percent of the commission's notices. . . . Across Wisconsin, 55 percent of individuals on the list lived in cities where Hillary Clinton beat Trump in 2016."

One of Trump's early initiatives was the creation, via executive order in May 2017, of a Presidential Advisory Commission on Election Integrity. He named Vice President Michael Pence as chair and Kris Kobach, secretary of state of Kansas, as co-chair.

Upon Kobach's appointment, *The Independent* newspaper noted that he had been "successfully sued four times for voter suppression." Writer Miles Mogulescu in the *Huffington Post* commented that "in choosing the co-chair of his new Commission on Election Integrity, Donald Trump just did the equivalent of appointing Vito Corleone to co-chair a commission on police corruption or Vladimir Putin to co-chair a commission on human rights."

Pence pledged the commission would "review ways to strengthen the integrity of elections in order to protect and preserve the principle of one person, one vote." But almost immediately, the commission's work became embroiled in controversy and suspicion. When the commission wrote to the fifty states, requesting personal information on voters, critics assumed the request had a nefarious purpose. Several states refused to comply, and even those that cooperated refused to provide all the information Kobach sought.

"Mr. Kobach will most likely use your data to make exaggerated claims about untold numbers of people who are supposedly registered and voting in multiple states," wrote Dale Ho, director of the ACLU's Voting Rights Project, in a *New York Times* commentary. "For years, he has operated an 'Interstate Crosscheck' system, which purports to compare voter rolls in about 30 states, in order to identify possible double registrants. This new endeavor looks like Crosscheck on steroids."

In January 2018, Trump dissolved the commission. Two commission members—Hans von Spakovsky and J. Christian Adams—wrote a piece for the *Washington Examiner* claiming the commission had been a victim of political sabotage. "Right off the bat, a third of the states flatly refused to give the commission the voter registration and voter history data we requested—even though it is supposed to be publicly available information." Spakovsky and Adams saw only two possible explanations: "either [those states] were part of the partisan 'resist-Trump-at-any-costs movement,' or they were afraid of what we might find." Also, they complained, "a swarm of meritless lawsuits, filed by progressive groups, hobbled our ability to make progress on our assignment. . . . The litigation strategy was to force our staff to devote all their time to responding to frivolous lawsuits, thereby sabotaging the commission's ability to function."

The Brennan Center for Justice, which was among the organizations that sued the commission, had a predictably different take: "This commission started as a tragedy and ended as a farce," the center's president, Michael Waldman, said. "It was a colossal waste of taxpayer money from the very beginning. It failed to find any evidence of the millions of illegal voters claimed by President Trump. But this should be more than just a somewhat-comic ending to a misguided effort. The claim of widespread voter fraud in the United States is, in fact, fraud. The demise of this commission should put this issue to rest."

The Washington Post editorialized that the commission was "predicated on the fabrication that American elections are rife with corruption. As the institutional embodiment of one of the president's more outlandish lies—that voter fraud accounted for Hillary Clinton having received 2.9 million more votes in the 2016 presidential election—the panel . . . convened just twice, was sued repeatedly, met with contempt from state election officials of both parties, had no impact on the conduct of elections and will be little missed." The *Post* lamented that the death of the commission would not stop Trump and other members of his party from continuing to make false claims about voter fraud. Those misleading assertions, pointed out the *Post*, continued to "provide a pretext to rationalize voter suppression."

• • •

Voter suppression did not begin with the Trump presidency. It has existed, in one form or another, since the Fifteenth Amendment theoretically removed "race, color, or previous condition of servitude" as justifications for denial of the vote. Voter suppression was the foundation on which the edifice of Jim Crow was built.

The Voting Rights Act of 1965 was designed to fight voter suppression. So suppressive initiatives got a major boost in 2013, when the Supreme Court aimed a wrecking ball at the Voting Rights Act.

The 5–4 opinion reached in *Shelby County v. Holder*, authored by Chief Justice John Roberts, demolished the provision that barred several southern states from changing their voting rules without the permission of the Justice Department. The presumption behind Roberts's ruling was that the US was no longer the racist country it had been in 1965. Back then, acknowledged Roberts, "extraordinary measures" were needed "to address an extraordinary problem." The US, he declared, was no longer divided in the same way, "yet the Voting Rights Act continues to treat it as if it were." It was time, he said, for the law to catch up with "current conditions."

In her dissent (joined by Stephen Breyer, Sonia Sotomayor, and Elena Kagan), Justice Ruth Bader Ginsburg bluntly dismissed Roberts's rosy analysis. Discrimination "still exists; no one doubts that," she wrote, yet "the Court today terminates the remedy that proved to be best suited to block that discrimination."

Of discrimination, she wrote, "Early attempts to cope with this vile infection resembled battling the Hydra. Whenever one form of voting discrimination was identified and prohibited, others sprang up in its place. This Court repeatedly encountered the remarkable 'variety and persistence' of laws disenfranchising minority citizens." Dr. Martin Luther King Jr. foresaw that "progress could be made even in Alabama, but there had to be a steadfast national commitment to see the task through to completion. . . . History has proved King right."

Ginsburg went on to note that Alabama, Mississippi, and other states continued to impede voting by persons of color. "Alabama's sorry history of violations alone provides sufficient justification" to keep the Voting Rights Act requirements in place. She concluded, citing Section 5 of the original act, that "it was the judgment of Congress that '40 years has not been a sufficient amount of time to eliminate the vestiges of discrimination following nearly 100 years of disregard for the dictates of the 15th amendment and to ensure that the right of all citizens to vote is protected as guaranteed by the Constitution.' . . . In my judgment, the Court errs egregiously by overriding Congress' decision."

Following the decision, the NAACP Legal Defense and

Educational Fund issued a statement slamming the Supreme Court for taking "the most powerful tool our nation has to defend minority voting rights out of commission." In 2019, on the sixth anniversary of the decision, the Congressional Black Caucus declared that states continued "to pass voter suppression laws that range from strict voter ID laws to the purging of voters from rolls."

In congressional testimony that June, Leah Aden of the NAACP Legal Defense and Educational Fund noted that since the 2013 Supreme Court ruling, "federal courts have found that officials in five different states have passed racially discriminatory voting laws intentionally—for the purpose of discriminating against Black and/or Latino voters. For example, in North Carolina, the Fourth Circuit Court of Appeals found that the legislature worked with 'surgical provision' to ensure that its omnibus voting law would disproportionately disenfranchise African American voters." She also cited suppression schemes in Texas, Kansas, and Wisconsin. In Alabama, she pointed out, officials purged voting rolls of scores of black students attending a historically black college in Madison County. "The transgressions in Alabama are disturbing," she testified, "but they are also indicative of a larger, nationwide trend [that] warrants attention."

• • •

Many experts see denial of the vote to felons who have served their time as another form of voter suppression. In 2019,

Common Cause released a report ("Zero Disenfranchisement: The Movement to Restore Voting Rights") arguing that felony disenfranchisement laws "not only have a disproportionate impact on communities of color and low-income communities, but also have no criminal deterrent or rehabilitative value." The report observed that the laws—which disenfranchise something over six million Americans—have a disgraceful history, and evoked Alabama's constitutional convention in 1901.

During his opening address, convention president John Knox talked up his plan to bolster white supremacy, which the white South considered to be under attack as a result of passage of the Fourteenth and Fifteenth Amendments. Those amendments respectively guaranteed all citizens, including the formerly enslaved, "equal protection of the laws" and granted the vote to males irrespective "of race, color, or previous condition of servitude." In order to nullify those new rights, why not simply prohibit convicted felons from voting, suggested Knox.

Knox's plan was simple, reported Common Cause. "If Alabama broadened its felony disenfranchisement law to include more crimes, then voting rights could be revoked in a seemingly nondiscriminatory way, especially since it was fairly easy to arrest and convict black men with little probable cause. The delegate who introduced the felony disenfranchisement provision, John Fielding Bums, stated, 'the crime of wife-beating alone would disqualify sixty percent of Negroes.' The general phrase 'moral turpitude' and crimes such as vagrancy, living in adultery, and wife-beating were all chosen for implementation of the law to target black people."

• • •

Some seventy years after the rise of the US civil rights movement, the country is in a fundamentally different place than it was in 1950. Most Americans think that in many ways we are in a better place. But Americans like Charlottesville's Jason Kessler have their doubts. They wonder, increasingly openly, whether the US is losing its identity, and many are prepared to use any weapon at their disposal to ensure that that does not happen.

That vocal and somewhat desperate minority seeks to cling to power by whatever means they can, even if that involves crossing ethical and legal lines. In a *New York Times* op-ed, political scientists Steven Levitsky and Daniel Ziblatt argued that the "greatest threat to our democracy today is a Republican Party that plays dirty to win."

They saw the decision by the Republican Senate to block Barack Obama from filling a Supreme Court vacancy in 2016 as part of a broader pattern: "After losing the governorship in North Carolina in 2016 and Wisconsin in 2018, Republicans used lame-duck legislative sessions to push through a flurry of bills stripping power from incoming Democratic governors. Last year, when the Pennsylvania Supreme Court struck down a Republican gerrymandering initiative, conservative legislators attempted to impeach the justices. And back in North Carolina, Republican legislators used a surprise vote last week, on Sept. 11, to ram through an override of Gov. Roy Cooper's budget veto—while most Democrats had been told no vote would be held."

Levitsky and Ziblatt concluded on a somber note: "Republicans won't abandon their white identity bunker strategy until they lose, but at the same time that strategy has made them so averse to losing they are willing to bend the rules to avoid this fate. There is no easy exit."

The decision to allow money to flood into politics, the decision to allow voter suppression to proceed with abandon, the decision to allow biased blather to preempt reasoned debate, all occurred in a context in which these were seen as winning strategies. But for how long? And at what cost?

9

DESTROYING DEMOCRACY, DEFENDING SPEECH

American exceptionalism is a point of national pride. The US is a nation greater than any other, with the oldest constitution of any functioning democracy on the planet. And because that constitution has served us so well, many of us see it as the equivalent of a secular Bible: a document crafted by geniuses incapable of creating a document containing serious flaws.

But although the Founders were indisputably brilliant, they were not granted the gift of foresight. They had no way of seeing—or imagining—a republic where, at the highest level of political power, truth is reviled and honor forsaken. They had no way of knowing that a process of selecting presidents, designed to elevate the best of the best, would degenerate into a system for consolidating power in the hands of amoral partisan hacks. They had no idea that the First Amendment—which was designed to enable the people to speak truth to power—would be hijacked by hatemongers, propagandists, and opportunists more interested in despoiling democracy and degrading debate than in ensuring that a diverse nation speaks in harmony.

The internet age has shown us that free expression can be poisonous. And it has forced a nation obsessed with the idea of freedom of speech to ask whether expression can be a bit too free.

After three years embedded in the world of internet trolls and "deplorables," author Andrew Marantz emerged with his idealism shaken. In the opening pages of *Antisocial: Online Extremists, Techno-Utopians, and the Hijacking of the American Conversation*, Marantz described his book as a story about "how a few disruptive entrepreneurs, motivated by naïveté and reckless techno-utopianism, built powerful new systems full of unforeseen vulnerabilities, and how a motley cadre of edgelords, motivated by bigotry and bad faith and nihilism, exploited those vulnerabilities to hijack the American conversation."

One truth Marantz discovered was how much emotions (often elicited by vile, hateful, and fabricated material) drive the culture and control the content of the internet. "High arousal emotions," as he called them, cause people to act—"in this case, clicking or liking or sharing a link." And that was the only type of emotion the viral internet values. Emotions that induce relaxation, torpor, or paralysis are useless—from a profit-making perspective: "From the standpoint of sheer entrepreneurial competition, what matters is not whether a piece of online content is true or false, responsible or reckless, prosocial or antisocial. All that matters is how many activating emotions it can provoke."

Shortly after the election of Donald Trump, Marantz interviewed prominent antifeminist blogger Michael Cernovich, who, as Wikipedia put it, "is known for his promotion of fake news." Cernovich insisted, "This election was a contest between PC [politically correct] culture and free-speech culture. Most people know what it's like for some smug, elite asshole to tell them, 'You can't say that, it's racist, it's bad.' Well, a vote for Trump meant, 'Fuck you, you don't get to tell me what to say.'"

Candidate Donald Trump reveled in the rise of this toxic, hateful culture. His ugly remarks and insults—whether trashing John McCain, a gold-star family, or the appearance of a political foe's wife—were part of what made Trump so compelling and watchable, and drove the press to lavish him with attention. He brought the ethos of the internet to traditional media. That was deeply ironic given he had leveraged the credibility of traditional media to convince people of the authenticity of the character he played on reality TV. After fourteen seasons playing the role of a super-smart, decisive, ultra-competent manager, he had millions of Americans convinced that was precisely what he was—and that made him the perfect candidate for a campaign based on polarizing emotions and a war on truth.

Even as the internet fueled the rise of the most bombastic

and openly bigoted president in the modern era, it facilitated an explosion of hate and violence that thrived in the new internet culture.

The incident with the largest number of victims occurred in Norway in 2011, when anti-immigration zealot Anders Behring Breivik killed seventy-seven people (some in an explosion, the rest by gunfire). Just before Breivik's killing spree, he released an online manifesto titled "2083: A European Declaration of Independence." The document, stretching to some 1,515 pages, praised conservative politicians and slammed Islam.

Since Breivik's rampage, we have seen a rash of mass killings that seem inspired by him and his fans. In 2019 in Christchurch, New Zealand, Brenton Tarrant, a twenty-eight-year-old described as a white supremacist, shot and killed fifty-one innocents—making it the deadliest mass shooting ever in New Zealand. He wounded another thirty-nine.

Although Tarrant and his sympathizers use the language of white supremacy, they seem less like people convinced of their superiority than of their vulnerability and victimhood. In a literal sense, they appear to be the opposite of supremacists—who presumably would be confident in their ability to overcome inferior beings by something short of shooting them. Instead, they seek encouragement and reassurance online. Their reaching out via accommodating internet sites (like his hero, Breivik, Tarrant also wrote an online manifesto) seems all about making their case to others who might feel sympathy for their suffering and therefore solidarity with their cause.

In its description of the Tarrant rant, Canada's *National Post* reported that "a manifesto was so important to [Tarrant], he wrote 240 pages and then, in a spasm of self-doubt, deleted it and began again, two weeks before his rampage. Or so claims the 74-page document Brenton Tarrant . . . allegedly released online shortly before the shooting started." The declaration, added the *Post*, "reads exactly like what it appears to be: the weaponization of the internet's culture of trolling, ranting, 'shitposts' and memes, the culmination of long, demoralizing hours watching online videos, reading anonymous forums, following conspiracy theories and conferring with selected Wikipedia entries. . . . He recounts his own radicalization to the white nationalist cause and encourages others to fan the flames of race war online through mimicking what he is himself mimicking in an echo chamber of racial violence."

The Christchurch manifesto directly pays tribute to the manifestos left by Anders Breivik as well as Dylann Roof, who in 2015 shot and killed nine blacks engaged in Bible study in a church in Charleston, South Carolina. Roof's online treatise was a screed disparaging blacks, Hispanics, Asians, and Jews. He wrote: "I chose Charleston because it is [the] most historic city in my state, and at one time had the highest ratio of blacks to Whites in the country. We have no skinheads, no real KKK, no one doing anything but talking on the internet. . . . [Someone] has to have the bravery to take it to the real world, and I guess that has to be me."

Patrick Crusius, a twenty-one-year-old accused of killing twenty-two people in El Paso, Texas, in 2019, also was apparently motivated by animus toward Hispanics. Like the others, Crusius posted a so-called manifesto, in which he expressed admiration for Tarrant, the Christchurch murderer. Echoing Donald Trump's rationale for a wall on the southern border, Crusius claimed he was defending his country from "cultural and ethnic replacement brought on by an invasion."

Less than a year before the shootings in El Paso, Robert Bowers, forty-five, attacked the Tree of Life synagogue in Pittsburgh. He yelled, "All Jews must die," and opened fire. His social network of choice was Gab, a site created in 2016 that promoted itself as a champion of free speech. Prior to his assault on the synagogue, Bowers had posted pictures of guns and warned that Jews were the "children" of Satan.

Terrorism analyst Rita Katz observed on *Politico*, "Gab's absolutist approach to speech—including what is often outright hate speech—has made the platform a safe haven for white supremacists and other far-right communities from all over the world." She added, "There is no hyperbole in calling Gab a cesspool of hateful and threatening rhetoric by 'Jew-wise people'—white supremacist code for anti-Semites. User names often contain Nazi insignia like swastikas and the Waffen-SS logo, while profiles promote 'anti-jew video podcasts' and websites 'advocating for the violent overthrow of the current ZOG.' Users post and repost messages stating 'kill them all' of the Jews and rap songs mockingly referencing gas chambers, just to name a few. As you scroll through profiles, passing the bounty of messages stating that Jews are 'human sewage' that 'must report to the oven' and 'all jews must die,' you feel as if you've stumbled into Hitler's Nazi Germany."

The murders at Tree of Life, Katz pointed out, had not prompted any apparent remorse: "Less than a day after news of the attack broke, many were celebrating on the platform. One user . . . posted a poll with the #treeoflifeshooting hashtag, asking, 'What should the future of Jewish people in the West be?' The answers were disturbing, with 35 percent voting for 'genocide.'"

Testifying before a Senate committee in September 2009, George Selim, senior vice president of programs for the Anti-Defamation League, argued that online forums such as Gab, 4chan, and 8chan "nurtured" murderers such as Bowers. In Selim's view, the internet had handed extremists a megaphone. It "amplifies the hateful voices of the few to reach millions around the world." And it allows lonely, isolated extremists to become players in a virtual network, where they can recruit like-minded souls around the world: "Individuals can easily find sanction, support, and reinforcement online for their extreme beliefs or actions, and in some cases neatly packaged alongside bomb-making instructions. This enables adherents like violent white supremacist mass shooters such as Bowers to self-radicalize without face-to-face contact with an established terrorist group or cell."

In reflecting on the mass murders in El Paso, Jonathan Bullington, an investigative reporter for Louisville's *Courier-Journal* wrote, "The simple truth, experts say, is that there is no one path toward domestic terrorism and no single profile of the perpetrators, although most are white males. . . . But most academics who study violent extremism agree the internet has exponentially extended the reach of hate groups, giving their ideologies nearly unfettered access to minds susceptible to their message."

Even before the internet became such a magnet for hate speech, people were using media for evil purposes. The genocidal mass slaughter in Rwanda in 1994 resulted in the deaths of an estimated 800,000 people, mostly Tutsis, in a span of a hundred days. Much of that killing was orchestrated and celebrated by radio broadcasts demonizing the Tutsis and demanding their destruction.

As Andrew Marantz pointed out in his *New York Times* op-ed, "The Clinton administration could have jammed the radio signals and taken those broadcasts off the air, but Pentagon lawyers decided against it, citing free speech. It's true that the propagandists' speech would have been curtailed. It's also possible that a genocide would have been averted."

The even more twisted irony is that the two leading offensive radio stations—Radio Rwanda and Radio Télévision Libre des Mille Collines—were government owned or controlled. In other words, if the United States was protecting free speech, it was not the speech of ordinary Rwandans but of a group of extremists within the Hutu-controlled government who took the occasion of the assassination of their president to orchestrate a genocide.

Is that what the First Amendment was meant to support: genocide by vindictive elements within a government? Did the Framers really believe that mentally ill individuals, motivated by hate, brought low by insecurity, and subject to murderous impulses, merited refuge in protected communities where their hate and sickness could be molded into terrorism?

• • •

In *The Soul of the First Amendment*, constitutional law expert Floyd Abrams observed that the "exceptionalism of the United States" leads it to be more protective of free speech than of such competing interests as equality, "personal privacy, and the need to safeguard national security."

Abrams also noted that in "an increasing number of cases . . . it has been the more conservative members of the Court who have been championing more expansive First Amendment protections. In those cases, more liberal jurists have not only differed with their conservative colleagues about the scope of the First Amendment but often taken positions that could more generally limit its impact."

In the end, Abrams comes down on the side of keeping free expression free, which means keeping the government out of the picture as much as possible. He argued, "No theoretical justification for protecting free expression provides any basis for ignoring the pervasive skepticism reflected in the First Amendment of governmental limits on or punishment of speech. Thomas Emerson, the patriarch of First Amendment scholars, has asserted as the first premise of . . . the 'system of freedom of expression' the proposition that the First Amendment serves the interest of 'assuring individual self-fulfillment'—which can only be achieved when one's mind is free. . . . The core teaching of the First Amendment is that those values are served best by limiting the power of government over speech, not augmenting it."

Elsewhere in the world, many distinguished thinkers see such absolutist—or rigid—thinking as absurd.

"What the right tends to want to do is to have rules that are hard and fast. 'This is unlawful. That is not unlawful.' 'There's freedom of speech, absolute.' And so on," Baroness Helena Kennedy, director of the International Bar Association's Human Rights Institute and a member of British Parliament, told me during an interview. She believes that rigidity leads to a false clarity, and while it eliminates the necessity to struggle with the complexity of the issue, it also leads, in her view, to bad decisions.

Kennedy has little patience with attempts to ban speech that simply causes "hurt feelings." That is "too difficult to police," among other things. But the question becomes harder when you consider potential terrorists: "I've done quite a lot of these cases representing radicals, radical Islamists." In considering whether to prohibit hate speech, the key question for her is "when [does] it cross a line?" When is speech "creating, if you like, the cultural backdrop from which violence is almost an inevitable next step?"

Determining that, she acknowledged, is a "difficult road." And complicating it is the fact that there is "a fertilizer quality in the internet now. It spreads this stuff much more effectively . . . a kind of multiplier of emotions that exist in all of our communities, and particularly when you have economic recession, or where you have things not working out as well for people."

• • •

In *Prospect* magazine in 2018, barrister Hugh Tomlinson published an article titled "Why It's Time for a British First Amendment to Protect Free Speech." The essence of his argument was that free speech is a "primary value" under the US Constitution, whereas Great Britain has no constitution and no similar protection, making speech protection subject to the whims of parliament: "Free speech does not, historically, have the same primacy under English law. Free speech is important but not decisive. The primacy of free speech is not compatible with the European Convention on Human Rights—a code written by British lawyers."

He also acknowledged that even if Great Britain did have a First Amendment, it would not protect all speech. "There is no easy way out of the difficult job of balancing rights on a case by case basis. The real value of such a provision [as a First Amendment] would be to require government, parliament, and the courts to defend and justify the imposition of any restrictions on free speech. Fundamental rights should not be casually disregarded."

During our interview, Tomlinson clarified that he did not see speech as a fundamental right. "In almost everywhere in the world, apart from the US, the way that fundamental rights protection works is there are some rights which can never be removed. The right not to be tortured, the right not to be held in slavery, those kinds of things. But most rights are what we call qualified rights. So they can be removed if it's necessary, if it's lawful, necessary, and proportionate. In our system, that includes . . . the right to freedom of assembly, the right to free speech, the right to privacy. These are qualified rights, which can be removed, but that removal has got to be justified. And the difficulty that we've had in Britain historically is we've got no rights protection at all. So the government can bring in legislation of an extreme nature, and has done from time to time, and there's no challenge to it."

Tomlinson also pointed out that in the United States there is no separating the issue of speech from the issue of wealth. Why, he asked rhetorically, does the US place such importance on freedom of speech but not on a right "you might think is hugely more important, the right to housing"? The reason, as he sees it, is that free speech cases are "basically brought by large, rich corporations, who are protecting their right to speak for their own commercial purposes. There are no large, rich corporations that are supporting the right of poor people to have houses. I think one of the challenges in democratic discourse is to ensure that those who have the loudest voice use it in a responsible way."

Tomlinson added that the First Amendment has never been absolute. Indeed, as I noted previously, for most of the life of this republic, the US has barely honored the First Amendment at all. And, as the very idea of fighting words makes clear, once we began to take the notion of free speech seriously, we still imposed limits on it—although we have loosened many of those limits through the years.

The angry outburst at a cop that got Jehovah's Witness Walter Chaplinsky arrested in New Hampshire in 1942 and led the Supreme Court to ruminate on the harm caused by so-called fighting words would scarcely raise an eyebrow today. There are considerably worse things you can be called than a racketeer or a Fascist. But the idea that speech has limits has never gone away.

When Floyd Abrams argued that the quest for "individual self-fulfillment" is a motivating rationale for the First Amendment, the ethos he invoked sounded more like something from the 1960s than from 1789, when the Bill of Rights was sent to the states. Indeed, the article he cited by Thomas Emerson ("the patriarch of First Amendment scholars") appeared in the *Yale Law Journal* in 1963. In that article, Emerson referenced "the great intellectual and social movement beginning with the Renaissance which transformed the Western world from a feudal and authoritarian society to one whose faith rested upon the dignity, the reason and the freedom of the individual."

Emerson went on to argue that "suppression of belief, opinion and expression is an affront to the dignity of man, a negation of man's essential nature. What Milton said of licensing of the press is equally true of any form of restraint over expression: it is 'the greatest displeasure and indignity to a free and knowing spirit that can be put upon him.' . . . To cut off his search for truth, or his expression of it, is thus to elevate society and the state to a despotic command and to reduce the individual to the arbitrary control of others." Emerson also invoked what he called the principle of equality: "formulated as the proposition that every individual is entitled to equal opportunity to share in common decisions which affect him."

Those are, without question, noble objectives. But many of those objectives seem to have little to do with how the Framers thought about free speech. Certainly, if they were primarily concerned with giving every individual a chance to equally share in decisions, they never would have countenanced either slavery or denying women the vote or even the Electoral College. And if the only point of the Bill of Rights was to allow each person the ultimate opportunity at "individual self-fulfillment," they no doubt would have considered Tomlinson's issue and endorsed a right to housing—and probably a right to employment as well. But they were building a nation, not a commune.

In 2019, writing in the *Harvard Journal of Law & Public Policy* ("The Sickness unto Death of the First Amendment"), Marc O. DeGirolami, a law professor at St. John's University School of Law, argued that the rationale for free speech was evolving. During the mid-twentieth century, he observed, many thinkers justified free speech by pointing to its value in fostering self-actualization or the fulfillment of potential. Later, he said, the right was seen as a bulwark against government value judgments and content-based restrictions—since free speech was considered "inherently good for the individual" and perhaps even an essential part of what it meant to be American. More recently, he asserted, the value of free speech was being weighed against other societal interests "such as democracy, dignity, equality, sexual autonomy, antidiscrimination, decency, and progressivism. For the new free speech constrictors, it is these other rights and interests, not free speech, that are the true or defining American civic goods."

The "free speech constrictors," as DeGirolami calls them, clearly make him nervous—and they probably should. Because for all the problems engendered by our current approach to speech—one that favors the wealthy and empowers hateful ideologues—no one has come up with a simple way of explaining how a more restrictive approach to speech would make things better.

Indeed, as DeGirolami made clear, those arguing for speech restrictions are likely to have agendas of their own. And as the ACLU concluded in the 1930s, when it published a pamphlet entitled *Shall We Defend Free Speech for Nazis in America?*, those agendas may ultimately render free speech null and void. The ACLU felt compelled to defend Nazis and equally loathsome characters because it saw no rational or consistent way to defend the right for good guys without also defending it for bad. Where, asked the ACLU, would one draw the line? Against those preaching racial or religious hatred? But how exactly is that defined? There "is no general agreement on what constitutes race or religious prejudice" or about who exactly is practicing it. Is it the Communists, the Socialists? Or is it atheists? Or perhaps "Jews attacking the Nazis"? Indeed, precisely because such laws might target Jews, the ACLU had defended bills outlawing Nazi propaganda. "No laws can be written to outlaw Nazi propaganda without striking at freedom of speech in general," concluded the ACLU.

That statement was written more than eighty years ago,

well before the internet offered a breeding ground for terrorists, long before so much money flooded into politics that it made the notion of "one person, one vote" laughable, and long before a determined political minority decided to dominate the political process into the foreseeable future by whatever measure—ethical or not—required to do so. It was written at a time when it was possible to believe that the quality of ideas was practically all that mattered in political debate and that truth eventually and inevitably conquered lies.

We no longer live in that world. In *Antisocial*, Andrew Marantz wonders what it means when traditional media gatekeeping has broken down, and when the "whole information ecosystem" seems to be in chaos.

One thing it undoubtedly means is that we must learn to let go of some of our absolutist illusions—which have never actually been true anyway. There was never a time in US history when free speech operated without constraints, when it was an absolute right. Government has always reserved the right to step in when it saw fit—although it has done so at times in a much more clumsy and ill-considered way than at others.

In an article published in 2016 in the *Columbia Law Review*, Erica Goldberg argued that courts already engage in what she called "free speech consequentialism," that they routinely try to determine whether speech's harms greatly outweigh its virtues. It is a practice, she added, courts should engage in only "sparingly, and should constrain themselves to considering only the harms caused by speech that can be analogized to harms caused by conduct."

Most Americans would probably agree that no one should go to prison for publicly declaring that they hate blacks, Jews, or rednecks, especially since anyone driven to shout such things is likely mentally challenged to begin with. But do they deserve the privilege of screaming such nonsense with a megaphone in the center of the public square? Is limiting their speech in any way really the first step to censoring speech in general?

Writing in the *Washington and Lee Law Review*, professor Lyrissa Barnett Lidsky pondered how society should respond to false factual information and Holocaust denial. She acknowledged that such things, despite their lack of value, enjoy "a measure of First Amendment protection" since the First Amendment "imposes something . . . of a presumption against government interference in public discourse. This presumption is rooted in suspicion of the State's ability to distinguish facts from falsehoods as well as its motives for doing so. However, the presumption against regulation of false speech is not absolute. It can be overcome when verifiably false speech poses a direct threat of harm to individual interests."

Does Holocaust denial represent such a harm? Lidsky admitted that despite "the very real threats posed by Holocaust denial," jurists generally don't see those harms as a sufficient reason to punish Holocaust deniers. She also accepted the argument that government "must tolerate a certain amount of false speech in order to protect true speech, especially where the line between truth and falsity is difficult to discern." But she questioned whether punishing "the most obvious and egregious forms of Holocaust denial' would really chill valuable speech. She doubted that it would, as there seems no more "to fear from State regulation of Holocaust denial than there is to fear from State regulation of obscenity or even defamation. Instead, the best reason to oppose punishment of Holocaust denial may be the pragmatic one. Since Holocaust denial is essentially a conspiracy theory, punishment of believers will only tend to strengthen their convictions. Moreover, it will drive them out of public discourse and into the echo chamber of like-minded believers on the internet. Punishment of Holocaust denial may therefore do little good, and unintentionally, much harm."

That is probably as good an argument as any for allowing Holocaust denial; but it is hardly a rationale for concluding government should do nothing about objectionable speech. That is a debate we, as a society, have yet to seriously hold—as is the discussion over speech rights and internet-based businesses.

There is a lot of territory between letting the government control speech and letting industry do whatever it wants (which is mostly to make money, even if that hurts people). And while it is extremely difficult to make a coherent argument that the government should willy-nilly limit scary speech, it is insane to pretend that we don't make trade-offs between various rights, including speech, all the time. In an age when private surveillance is already pervasive and sectors of the internet have become a breeding ground for violent notions, it is imperative that we come up with effective interventions in providing mental health remedies and in preventing violence. But it is also important to sort out whether we have the balance right when it comes to how speech is treated on the internet—and in society in general. As Baroness Kennedy pointed out, there will be challenges and difficulties down that road, which does not mean it is a discussion to be avoided.

But our problem as a democracy is not just a speech problem; it is that a significant part of our republic rejects democratic values, which, after all, is what free speech is supposed to protect. That sector of the US apparently fears a diverse electorate so much that it will use whatever means are at its disposal to suppress many Americans' ability to vote—even if that means turning a blind eye to foreign intervention, supporting a president who embraces an enemy of the United States, and polarizing the country to such an extent that democracy itself may be endangered.

There are moments when I wonder whether some future historian will look back on one of the greatest civilizations in the history of the world and lament that, even as we debated the importance of free speech, we forgot that free speech was supposed to have a purpose, that it was supposed to be a means of defending our freedoms and our republic—not of facilitating our self-destruction. In losing sight of that idea, we may be unwittingly killing free speech, not in any literal sense but as an ideal, even as we abandon the fantasy that embracing free speech was necessarily tantamount to safeguarding this country's soul.

EPILOGUE

A VIRUS, PARTISANSHIP, AND TRUTH

In this, the age of the coronavirus pandemic, one country, one continent after another, has been brought low by a foe we never saw coming. Nothing like an old-fashioned, world-changing pandemic to drive home our inherent vulnerability—and reveal our chronic shortsightedness.

As frightening as COVID-19 is, it has given us images of inspiration: Italians singing their national anthem in unison from their balconies, New Yorkers pausing nightly to collectively cheer nurses and other caregivers, distilleries using their equipment to produce hand sanitizer, volunteers shopping for elderly strangers. The tragedy also has compelled us to wrestle with some hard truths; and it has forced those of us in the United States to grapple with how paralyzingly divided our country is.

Of all the scary statistics I have seen in the wake of the pandemic, one of the most depressing was produced by the Marist Poll. "Do you trust the information you hear about the coronavirus from President Trump?" asked the pollsters. Seventy-four percent of Republicans trusted the president's words "a great deal" or "a good amount." Only eight percent of Democrats believed the president at all.

Put another way, Republicans were more than nine times as likely as Democrats to accept the president's view on how to respond to a potentially fatal virus. We are not talking here about the natural partisanship you would expect to find on political issues—such as whether Medicare is good or privatization of the postal service is bad. We are talking, quite literally, about an issue of life or death, in which following bad advice could kill. We also are talking of a president who has a proven record as a prevaricator. During the early stages of the outbreak, he consistently downplayed the seriousness of the threat. He assured us, "Like a miracle, it will disappear"; "We're very close to a vaccine"; "We closed it down; we stopped it." And those assurances, all falsehoods, were called out promptly and loudly by the press.

Nonetheless, and despite the fact that following Trump's lead increased the odds of disease and death, most of his party members went along—including an array of Republican governors who rejected social distancing guidelines recommended by experts in deference to Trumps' blasé outlook. Please take a moment to take that in. Some people, thanks to their party affiliation, cared more about standing with Trump than standing up for life.

Partisanship has always been a part of politics. But there is something different—and frightening—about this moment in which partisanship nullifies the warnings of science and the ability to accept reality. Obviously, we have never before had a president so determined to tear down the institutions he was charged with leading, or so filled with anger at a so-called deep state purportedly intent on taking him down. Trump is exceptionally gifted at driving people apart, in shutting out a large part of the population, as he rallies his people around him. While that may be a great strategy for unifying a base, it is no way to unify a nation—and certainly not in a time of crisis, when the entire country should be pulling together.

If that was ever unclear, it became painfully obvious in May 2020, as the public wrestled not just with a terrible epidemic but with the spectacle of a white cop recorded choking a handcuffed black man to death. As violence raged in American cities, Trump tweeted a warning invoking the memory of the suspect killed in custody: "These THUGS are dishonoring the memory of George Floyd, and I won't let that happen. Just spoke to Governor Tim Walz and told him that the Military is with him all the way. Any difficulty and we will assume control but, when the looting starts, the shooting starts. Thank you!" Twitter tagged the post, noting, "This Tweet violated the Twitter Rules about glorifying violence. However, Twitter has determined that it may be in the public's interest for the Tweet to remain accessible."

The *Miami Herald* and other newspapers promptly pointed out that Trump's threat echoed the words of Miami's former police chief Walter Headley, whose 1967 response to crime in black neighborhoods was, "when the looting starts, the shooting starts," and who had pledged to use shotguns and dogs to whip black hoodlums into line. Instead, Headley's "aggressive policies . . . led to violence," reported the *Herald*.

Where Trump saw an opportunity to foster anger and rile those eager to answer chaos with escalating violence, countless others saw an opportunity to scream a united, "Enough!" They showed up at rallies across America to say they were tired not just of the needless deaths of people like George Floyd but also of the lies and flawed assumptions that justified such murders. It was perhaps time, they suggested, to get beyond some of what divides us, to perhaps work toward a commitment to a collective truth that will let us save our country and preserve this planet.

In January 2020, *The Atlantic* magazine asked, "When truth itself feels uncertain, how can a democracy be sustained?" Even if more than 40 percent of Americans accept Trump's version of truth, that is not enough to make a virus disappear. It is not enough to make the globe start cooling down, or to erase the wealth inequality that threatens to destabilize whole societies. It won't turn murderous dictators into America's best friends.

Bigotry, nationalism, bravado, and falsehoods will take you only so far. But maybe that is far enough for a man whose most devout desire is apparently the humiliation of anyone who ever made him feel small. Maybe, for such a person, successfully waging war on truth is the best revenge. And maybe, for his most fervent supporters, truth is an overrated virtue. Maybe, for his base, the joy of having intolerance affirmed is worth the loss of the world.

But what about those unwilling to accept false "truths" marinated in self-justifying bigotry? What, in other words, is the responsibility of those disempowered citizens who happen to belong to the too silent but actual majority?

Clearly, part of that previously silent majority finally has found a voice. Suddenly, despite the restrictions imposed by a lethal pandemic, millions rose up, uniting to share a pain and outrage that demanded togetherness in a time of distance. And the world trembled.

It is a rising up unlike anything America has seen in generations; and it remains unclear what the awakening has wrought. But it is clear that a lot of people have reached a breaking point and are speaking out against the lies and self-serving justifications that allowed the country, for so long, to turn away, to ignore the voices that whispered and then screamed, for generations, "I can't breathe."

The phrase has now become an anthem—a chant that evokes the memory of others who died for the crime of being disdained. It is a mantra forcing us to face unpleasant truths that the nation has long denied, a prayer that calls out to the best in us instead of the worse, a cry that unites people—diverse in color, age, experience, and privilege—willing to challenge unexamined assumptions in the quest for a way to live together in respect and harmony.

In May 2020, the world trembled; and the aftershocks will be felt for quite some time and may, indeed, signify the birth of a movement serious about fighting for the salvation of our troubled world.

ACKNOWLEDGMENTS

As a lifelong journalist, I have always had a special reverence for the First Amendment and for the essential and prominent role it assigned the press. Like many journalists, I had taken *New York Times v. Sullivan* as something close to sacred text. That 1964 Supreme Court decision had slapped down southern segregationists out to destroy the civil rights movement and, along with it, the free American press. With that decision, I assumed, the high court had forever ensured that the nation's free press would protect vulnerable Americans from the tyranny of powerful interests.

I was wrong.

During my stint as writer in residence for the ACLU, I had plenty of time to think through the many ways in which I was wrong. I thank Anthony Romero and Dorothy Ehrlich for giving me that opportunity. I also thank the University of California, and its National Center for Free Speech and Civic Engagement, which named me among its inaugural fellows, for providing an environment in which to further develop the ideas that make up the core of this book.

I owe a huge debt of gratitude to Tracy Sherrod, my brilliant editor, and Judith Curr, my prescient publisher, who immediately saw merit in what I was trying to do and warmly offered their support on the basis of little more than a pleasant conversation. I thank my agent, Don Fehr, for his encouragement and support, and the renowned constitutional lawyer Marty Garbus for his thoughtful and fervent cheerleading. I thank my wife, Lee, and my daughter, Elisa, for their boundless faith and unwavering devotion.

For any errors or omissions this book may contain, I have only myself to blame.

ABOUT THE AUTHOR

Ellis Cose is the author of a dozen books on issues of national and international concern, including the bestseller *The Rage of a Privileged Class.* Cose, a widely respected journalist, has served as writer in residence for the ACLU, columnist and contributing editor of *Newsweek*, editorial page chief for the *New York Daily News*, a fellow at the National Research Council of the National Academy of Sciences, a fellow of the Joint Center for Political and Economic Studies, a fellow of the Gannett Center for Media Studies at Columbia University, a fellow of the National Center for Free Speech and Civic Engagement of the University of California, and a contributor and columnist for numerous other major publications, including *USA Today* and *TIME.* Cose has appeared on *The Today Show, Nightline, Dateline, ABC World News Tonight, Good Morning America*, PBS's *Time to Choose* election special, *Charlie Rose*, CNN's *Talkback Live*, and a variety of other national and local televised programs. He lives in New York City.